Which? Way to Complain

WHICH?
WAY TO
COMPLAIN

Ian Cooper

Published by Consumers' Association
and Hodder & Stoughton

Published in Great Britain by Consumers' Association
14 Buckingham Street, London WC2N 6DS
and Hodder & Stoughton Limited
47 Bedford Square, London WC1B 3DP

Scottish consultants: Hamish Henderson and James Woodward-Nutt
Northern Irish consultant: Basil Glass

Illustrations by Simon Gooch
Cover design by Andrew Kay

Revised edition
© 1984 Consumers' Association

ISBN 0 340 35104 7

Filmset in England by
Rowland Phototypesetting Ltd
Bury St Edmunds, Suffolk
Printed by Spottiswoode Ballantyne Ltd
Colchester, Essex, and London

Contents

5

CONTENTS

Introduction

Most people find themselves at some time or another with complaints against a variety of different people, bodies and groups about an equally varied number of problems. In many cases, although an individual's legal rights have been infringed, or he has suffered some serious injustice perhaps as a result of incompetence or 'maladministration', he is either reluctant to complain or simply doesn't know how or where to go to resolve the complaint or dispute. This book is for such people. It sets out to provide guidance about when to complain, to whom, and how best to make the complaint. It examines a number of situations where complaints frequently arise, and suggests ways in which a person may help himself to resolve the difficulty in the most effective and least troublesome way. It is not essentially a legal rights book, but it does provide down-to-earth guidelines as to how you can go about protecting your rights.

The book gives guidance on what to do if you live in England or Wales. Where complaints procedures differ in Scotland or Northern Ireland, a raised number indicates that you should turn to the end of the chapter for more information.

General rules about complaining

Only complain when it is necessary

A vast number of people never complain even when they would be thoroughly justified in doing so. On the other hand there is another group who seem to have endless time and resources to complain about the most trivial of matters.

Complaining is not a pastime, nor is it a profession. Examine your conscience and complain only when it is necessary. This book sets out to explain how a justifiable complaint may be drawn to the attention of the proper body or person, so that the issue can be dealt with most effectively. It is not meant to encourage the 'professional complainer'. In short, complain by all means when you have something to complain about **but** don't enjoy it too much.

Give the party you are complaining about a chance to sort things out first

This book maps out a choice of routes for pursuing a genuine complaint. But before jumping in at the deep end and sending out letters to MPs, Ministers and the Queen, give the person or body at the brunt of your complaint a chance to voice their side of the case and to put things right first. This will probably save everyone a lot of wasted time and aggravation.

Complain to the right person

If you are going to the trouble of making a complaint, make it to a person in a position to do something about it. There is little point, for example, in complaining to a British Rail porter that the crisps you bought on the 7.57 from Inverness were soggy. Enquire to whom you should make the complaint, then contact them in person, by appointment or by letter.

Don't lose your temper, swear or get personal

Adopting the right tone is extremely important in making a successful complaint. Be polite but firm and confident. You want the party to whom you are complaining to recognise how reasonable you are being. If he thinks you are a belligerent so-and-so he will treat you accordingly.

Know your rights

In many cases the basis of your complaint is that your legal rights have been infringed, so a basic knowledge of what these are can be very helpful.

Weigh up what you have to gain

Sometimes it is important to be aware that even if you are able to establish that your complaint is justified, in practice you will have gained very little for yourself. For example, if you successfully establish a complaint against the police you might get a letter of apology. Or if you manage to prove that a lawyer or an architect is guilty of some professional misconduct he might only be formally reprimanded. If you are going to be happy with such results by all means go ahead. After all, it is only by making such complaints, often based on a matter of principle, that standards can be maintained or improved for the sake of everyone.

Complain in writing

Wherever practical, make your complaint in writing, preferably on a typewriter. There's not much point in complaining at all if the other person can't read your handwriting. Keep your letter polite, business-like, reasonably formal and concise, and **take and keep copies**.

Keep correspondence and other documents

Try to keep all correspondence and documentation relating to your complaint or to something which could possibly result in a dispute some time in the future: for example, letters, estimates, invoices, receipts. Attempt to have them clean and readily available.

Be patient

Even the simplest of complaints will take time to resolve, particularly if you are dealing with a big organisation. Some disputes may involve a lengthy correspondence and the whole issue take several months or even more than a year. So don't start unless you have got the patience and the stomach to see it through.

Give credit where credit is due and say thank you

It never does any harm to give credit to those who have provided a good and helpful service. Saying thank you can go a long way to making sure that good services or facilities remain of that quality.

Complaints about goods

COMPLAINTS ABOUT UNSATISFACTORY GOODS

A typical example: you buy a pair of shoes in a sale. A week later one of the straps comes right away making the shoes unwearable. What should you do?

Although there is no obligation on you to return the goods, it would be a good idea to take them back as soon as you discover the defect. Alternatively, you could offer to send them by post as long as the charges are reimbursed. If it is totally impracticable for you to return to the shop at once, perhaps because you live a long way off and transport is difficult, or because the goods are heavy or bulky, telephone or write to say that you are dissatisfied with the product and ask for collection arrangements to be made. Any unexplained or unreasonable delay may weaken your case.

Many people believe that the initial complaint about faulty goods should be made to the manufacturer. This is **not** the case. Your deal is with the retailer, the party who sold you the goods, and so it is to him that your complaint should be made.

How to complain

Make your complaint to the right person
It is always a good idea to ask for the manager in a shop or the departmental manager in a large store. Shop assistants are not usually authorised to deal with complaints especially if there is a question of a refund. In asking for a person in authority you also show that you mean business right from the start. Don't be fobbed off with the common response that the manager is 'in a meeting' or 'away'. Insist that someone must have been left in charge and that you'll see that person. Failing that, register your complaint with the assistant and make an appointment to call back and see the manager at a mutually convenient time.

If you do agree to call back on another occasion you may be asked to leave the goods so that the manager has time to inspect them. This is not wholly unreasonable on the shop's part, but as a general guideline try to avoid leaving goods behind. If you decide to leave the goods with the shop, make sure you get a receipt and ask them to write on it 'for inspection only'. This may prevent a dispute later arising from an allegation that you left the goods for repair.

Be polite but firm

When making your complaint it is important that you adopt the right tone. The last thing you want to do is deliberately antagonise the person you are dealing with, so avoid losing your temper, shouting, swearing and making threats. You want to come over as a reasonable sort of person, and if you act reasonably the chances are that the other person will deal with you in a reasonable manner too. You should try to be polite but firm and to give a generally businesslike impression.

Be wary of starting out with the right tone but finishing up by creating an embarrassing scene and having a row in a shop full of people. This is almost guaranteed to get you nowhere. Once the other person has adopted a certain stance it is highly unlikely that you will change his mind by verbal assault, and anyway you may say something in the heat of the moment which you will regret later on.

Know what you want

It is remarkable how many people return faulty products to the seller not having the faintest idea what they want to happen. Determined customers have taken back goods prepared to do battle, only to be floored by the question: 'Well, what would you like us to do about it?' Do you want a full refund, a repair, a credit note or an exchange? You may not get what you want but you should decide beforehand.

Take a receipt

Wherever possible try to take your receipt back with the goods. You should always make sure, of course, that you get receipts for anything you buy and that you look after them well. Everyone knows that in practice this is virtually impossible as many receipts are barely legible scraps of paper and very easily lost. The main purpose of being able to produce a receipt is to prove that the goods were purchased from that particular shop or store. It is perfectly reasonable that the seller should question that the goods were bought from him before he takes steps to rectify your complaint. However, not having a receipt does not mean that you should forget the whole business. You may be able to give proof of purchase in some other way: for example, you may have a cheque stub or credit card voucher, or a particular trader's name may be stitched or stamped on to the product, or the assistant who sold you the goods may remember you, or you may have had someone with you when you bought the goods. As far as the law is concerned you don't have to have a receipt but in practice it helps.

Give credit where credit is due and say thank you.

Know the law

Knowing your legal rights can be an enormous help as it is bound to give you confidence and more often than not put you in a stronger bargaining position than you would be in otherwise. At its simplest the law you need to know is that every time you buy goods, even second-hand goods, from a shop, mail order catalogue, indeed from any business, you enter into a contract with the seller. Under this contract the law places upon both parties a number of obligations. The most important obligations that the seller owes you, the buyer, are laid down in the Sale of Goods Act 1979. The obligations are:

- that the **seller owns the goods**
- that the goods **correspond with any description given**
- that the goods are of **merchantable quality**
- that the goods are **fit for their purpose**

Description

If any description is applied to the goods, part of the contract is that the goods will match that description. For example, if the colour or size of an item is specified on its box the item must be of that colour or size. Otherwise the seller will be in breach of contract and you can insist on a refund.

Merchantable quality

Being of merchantable quality means that the goods will be fit to do the job that you would reasonably expect of goods of that type, taking into account their price, age and so on. So a washing machine must wash, food be fit to be eaten and shoes fit to be worn, regardless of whether or not they were bought in a sale. If goods are not of merchantable quality, the seller will have broken his part of the contract and is obliged to take the goods back, to give a full refund and to compensate the customer for any loss suffered as a result of the product's defect. For example, if a faulty tumble drier damages a number of items of clothing the customer will be entitled to compensation for any reasonable loss suffered as a result of the fault, as well as a full refund of the purchase price of the tumble drier. The shop may offer an exchange, a repair or a credit note instead of the full refund but where goods are not of 'merchantable quality' and you agree to anything other than a refund you are accepting less than you are entitled to. Again, you should make up your mind about what you are prepared to accept before you return to the shop.

Fitness for purpose

If you bought an item for a specific purpose, made that purpose known to the seller and then acted on his recommendation, this too is part of your contract – that the goods will be fit for the purpose you made known. For example, if you seek the advice of an assistant in a hardware shop about the type of glue to stick

wood together and he recommends a particular one, then if the glue does not in practice do the job the seller is in breach of contract and you are entitled to a refund. Note that these legal rights are against the seller of the goods by virtue of your contract with him, despite any manufacturer's guarantee.

Summary It is important to recognise that you are only entitled to these rights if some contractual obligation has been broken by the seller. You do not have the right to insist on anything if you simply decide you don't like what you have bought, for example because of the price, size or colour. A customer who buys a sweater to go with a shirt bought some time ago has no right to return the sweater for a refund upon discovering that the two items don't look good together. This is not a justifiable complaint although in order to retain good customer relations the shop may go beyond what they have to do and give a refund or change the goods. Bear in mind too that the legal obligations are exactly the same if you are buying the goods on credit, such as in a hire purchase deal, although in some circumstances you may have the additional right to take up the matter with any finance company involved.

All these rights apply provided the goods were bought from a business. If they were bought privately, for instance through the small ads column of a local newspaper or from a neighbour, the goods do not have to be of merchantable quality or fit for their purpose but they still have to be as they are described.

14

Responses to your complaint

Following the basic guidelines for complaining about defective goods, here are a number of typical responses with suggestions for dealing with them.

We'll give you a full refund

When you return faulty goods to the seller, don't **expect** to encounter problems. If your complaint is reasonable the majority of shops or traders will either offer you your money back or replace or repair the object. After all, the good will of the customer is extremely important to a trader. Indeed for this reason many large department stores will give a full refund even if the goods are not defective and even though they are not under any legal obligation to give you anything.

It may be that you don't want a refund but an exchange. What then? Perhaps the item you bought was in a sale and a refund of the sale price would not enable you to buy a similar item elsewhere. If this is the case you must simply regard yourself as unlucky and take the refund. You have no legal right to insist on an exchange, which may anyway be impossible if the shop has no more of that particular model or size in the sale.

We'll exchange

Very often a shop will offer a dissatisfied customer an exchange. This way they retain the customer's money and good will, and can then take the matter up with their supplier in the hope that they in turn can be reimbursed for buying faulty goods. But you are under no legal obligation to accept an exchange. If you want a refund since the goods are not up to the standards imposed by law on the seller, he has broken his contract with you, and you can and indeed should insist on a refund.

We'll give you a credit note

Instead of a refund or an exchange, a shop will occasionally offer a credit note. This amounts to a voucher for a particular sum, the price you paid for the goods, which can only be spent in that shop or at another branch of the same firm. An offer of a credit note is very much third best and as a rule should be rejected. If you have been offered a credit note because the goods are defective you should politely refuse to accept it, pointing out that you are prepared to insist on your legal right to a full refund. If you do accept a credit note remember that you can't change your mind about it afterwards. Make sure it's undated or at least long-term.

Give the person or body you are complaining about a chance to voice their side of the case and to put things right first. This will probably save everyone a lot of wasted time and aggravation.

Send them back to the manufacturer. We only sold them. They made them, not us

This response is unfortunately all too common, when perhaps a sales assistant in ignorance tries to pass on to the manufacturer what is the trader's own responsibility. Don't fall into this trap. It is up to the seller, the person with whom you have the contract, to put things right: any other suggestion should be rejected and the seller informed of his legal responsibility.

It's still under the manufacturer's guarantee – it must be repaired under that

Of all the responses given to an unhappy customer this is by far the most common. Many assistants and traders genuinely believe this is the extent of their obligations. Unfortunately, too many customers are prepared to accept the response. It is a legal nonsense – you should tell the seller that your main rights are against him, not the manufacturer, and that it is he who should put matters right.

What then is the use of the manufacturer's guarantee? The answer is that it gives the customer a choice over whether to send the goods back under the guarantee, or whether to take up the dispute with the seller. If you feel that the latter is likely to prove troublesome you may decide to make use of the manufacturer's guarantee. In other words, the guarantee is not in place of your legal rights, it is in addition to them. Look at any guarantee: it will say something on the lines of 'statutory rights unaffected'.

Consider the implications of accepting the response of 'Send it back under the guarantee'. You may resent the idea that the shop has the benefit of your money while you are without the use of the goods. But to send the goods back under the guarantee may turn out to be the lesser of two evils as far as inconvenience to you is concerned. For one thing a guarantee represents certainty, especially where the seller is digging his heels in and insisting that the goods were of merchantable quality. Again, if for instance the switch that operates the oven light breaks down you would hardly expect your money back from the shop on the whole cooker. A free repair to the switch by the manufacturer would probably be quicker and therefore less inconvenient to you than one carried out by the shop, simply because there is a system set up for such repairs. In any case goods returned under guarantee are often replaced by the manufacturer.

If you do decide to make use of the manufacturer's guarantee, here are a couple of practical suggestions:

■ Ask the shop to lend you another item of the same type while yours is being repaired. For example, the item in question might be a camera which you bought specifically to take on holiday and to be without it would be extremely disappointing. The shop does not have to lend you an item but it may do so simply in the interests of good customer relations. If it refused and the camera's faults were such that you eventually claimed your money back, you would be entitled to add on a quantifiable sum for loss of use, so again the shop is likely to lend you a replacement.

■ Write a letter to the shop saying that you are prepared to send the goods back under the manufacturer's guarantee, but that you nevertheless reserve your statutory rights to a refund should the action at the manufacturer's prove unsatisfactory. This is the sort of letter to write:

Dear Sir [*or name of manager*]   [*Date*]

I am writing to you regarding a Click Faster camera I bought from your shop on May 10, 1983 priced £110.

On attempting to use the camera for the first time I discovered that the shutter was broken and it was therefore incapable of taking photographs. I am writing to inform you that while I am sending the camera back to the manufacturers under their guarantee, I am formally reserving the right to reject the goods under my Sale of Goods Act rights and to claim a full refund if the manufacturers prove unable to provide a satisfactory solution within a reasonable time, or if a further problem arises.

Yours faithfully

[*Yours sincerely, if manager's name used*]

There is one situation where a manufacturer's guarantee can prove invaluable – when you have received the goods as a gift. As the recipient you will have no contract with the seller of the item and therefore no Sale of Goods Act rights; the guarantee is your only hope.

Nothing we can do, your guarantee has expired
This is another extremely common response to customers' complaints over faulty goods. It should be clear by now that the guarantee has nothing to do with your legal rights. Therefore the trader cannot legitimately use this excuse to escape liability. The Sale of Goods Act 1979 says that the goods must be of merchantable quality when you buy them, and in addition to this the courts have said that the goods must remain of merchantable quality 'for a reasonable length of time'. Obviously what is reasonable will vary according to the type of goods, their price and age and so on. Certain foods, for example, might be expected to remain fit for their purpose for only a matter of days, whereas a washing machine might stay so for a few years, and shoes at least several months depending on the type of wear. There is no real guide except perhaps your own common sense. If you genuinely believe that the item should have remained of merchantable quality for longer, you have the right to a refund.

17

We'll repair it for you free of charge

The shop may offer you a free repair. If the goods are not of merchantable quality you do not have to accept this and can insist on a refund. If you do decide to accept a repair you are accepting less than you are entitled to, so it would be a good idea to write to the retailer telling him that if you find the repair is not done to your complete satisfaction you will reserve your statutory rights to a refund.

We don't give refunds or exchanges without a receipt

This too is quite a common response. A receipt operates only as proof of purchase and it is obviously not unreasonable that the shop should want proof that you bought the product from them before they offer some sort of remedy. However, if you have not got or have lost your receipt, you can prove that you bought the item from them by some other means (see earlier in the section, under the heading **Take a receipt**). If the shop refuse to put things right on the grounds that you do not have a receipt and you have no other proof of purchase, any case you have against the trader is substantially weakened. You have only one weapon – the fact that the shop may want to preserve your good will and not get involved in a dispute over what may well be a small sum of money. You should appeal to the shop on that basis, first orally, then if unsuccessful in writing. Send a letter like this:

Dear Sir [*or manager's name or managing director*]   [*Date*]

I am writing to you concerning a pair of soft bedroom slippers I bought from your shop two weeks ago for £3.75.

Within two days of perfectly normal wear the heels on both slippers came apart. I returned to the shop with the defective slippers and explained what had happened. Unfortunately as I had lost the receipt I was told that no refund or exchange could be given.

I am writing to you to give you my formal assurance that the slippers were bought from your shop. I can only appeal to you that on the basis of good will and customer relations you will reconsider the position and offer me a refund or an exchange.

Yours faithfully [*Yours sincerely, if manager's name used*]

Sorry, we don't give refunds – look at the notice on the wall

Signs such as 'No refunds given' used to be extremely common. They are gradually disappearing thanks to fairly recent legislation but can still be seen in some places. The Unfair Contract Terms Act 1977 makes such signs totally invalid so you should ignore them and insist on your legal rights. Furthermore not only are such notices legally worthless, but displaying them is now a criminal offence. Knowing this can be a useful weapon in any dispute. The trader may think that such a sign still carries some weight, or, if he **is** aware of the legal position, he may be relying on the ignorance of the customer. However there are a number of variations of 'No refunds given' – some are valid and some not.

■ **Refunds or exchanges cannot be given on sale goods**
If the goods were bought in a sale and were not of merchantable quality, this sign is invalid and illegal, providing you did not know about or did not have pointed out to you the defect at the time of the purchase. Your legal rights are the same as if you had paid the full price. The goods must conform to the standards laid down by the Sale of Goods Act; otherwise a breach of contract will have taken place and a full refund should be given. Don't be fobbed off with this response – you know your rights, insist politely on having them.

■ **Customers please note – in no circumstances will a refund be considered other than in those which take into account current consumer legislation**

This one is valid and legal but morally dubious. 'Current consumer legislation' tells the customer that he still has all his Sale of Goods Act rights, but the notice is worded so as to intimidate or mislead him into believing that his rights have been taken away.

The goods were fine when you took them: you must have caused the damage

The basis of this response is that the goods were of merchantable quality when you bought them but that you have done something to cause the very defect you are complaining of. You insist that you have done nothing. One way to resolve the argument is to sue the shop and let the Court decide between the two parties. Another, and perhaps a better, way at this stage is to submit the product for independent testing by an appropriate trade association, providing of course the shop you bought the goods from is a member of that association. See page 25 for more details.

You do not have to use this method of complaining but it can be cheaper and perhaps less worrying than going to Court. If you do decide to make use of a trade association's complaints procedure and you are not satisfied with the result, in some circumstances you can still go to Court (see page 27).

Taking the complaint further

You've returned the faulty goods to the shop but have had to leave without a satisfactory response. What do you do next? From this point, you continue your complaint in writing. Send a formal letter of complaint to the manager of the shop, and take two copies, one to keep for yourself and another to send to the shop's head office later if necessary. The contents of this, and indeed of almost all first letters of complaint, can be broken down into four identifiable paragraphs/sections.

PARAGRAPH 1   Introduce yourself, and given details of your purchase: what it is, colour, size, model no., date of purchase, receipt no., and price

PARAGRAPH 2   State what is wrong with the product. You don't have to go into technical details but try to be specific

PARAGRAPH 3   Remind the shop of its legal obligations under the Sale of Goods Act 1979, and state that you are cancelling your contract

PARAGRAPH 4   Tell the shop what you want it to do, eg look into the matter, give a refund, etc

To give an example: imagine you've recently bought a tumble drier which has suddenly refused to work at all after three weeks of perfectly normal use. You've been into the shop to complain and have been given the 'send it back to the manufacturer under the guarantee' excuse. This is the sort of letter you should write (preferably type):

[Date]

Dear Sir *[manager's name if known]*,

PARAGRAPH 1 I am writing to you concerning a Dry-Faster Tumble Drier, model no. 2851, that I bought from your shop on *[date]*, priced £215.95, receipt no. 00713.

PARAGRAPH 2 After three weeks of normal use the tumble drier suddenly ceased working altogether. The Dry-Faster repairers called to examine the machine and discovered that the motor had been fitted to the machine incorrectly, and that this had caused damage to other parts of the tumble drier. They said that to repair the machine would be a lengthy job. When I called into the shop to explain the circumstances I was told 'It's not our responsibility – you'll have to send it back under the manufacturer's guarantee.'

PARAGRAPH 3 Given the facts as I have outlined, I must remind you of your legal obligations. The Sale of Goods Act 1979 states that goods sold must be of merchantable quality. Clearly the tumble drier I purchased is not, so I am formally cancelling my contract with you.

PARAGRAPH 4 As you are in breach of your legal obligations under that Act, I am entitled to a full refund of £215.95, and this is what I am seeking. Would you also please arrange for the tumble drier to be removed? I look forward to hearing from you within a fortnight.

Yours faithfully *[Yours sincerely, if manager's name used]*

[your signature]

[your name clearly written or typed]

Responses to your letter

It is likely that your letter will bring about one of three responses

- An apologetic letter informing you that they will give you a full refund or generally concede to your demands.
- They will refuse to give you a refund by telling you why they should not. It is likely that they may reiterate the 'send it back to the manufacturers under the guarantee' excuse that you were given initially in the shop. The letter would say something like this:

[*Date*]

Dear Mrs Sharp

Thank you for your letter of [*date*] regarding the tumble drier you bought from us.

While we very much regret the difficulties you have encountered with your machine we feel unable to make any refund to you. The machine is still under guarantee and we would therefore advise you to take advantage of it and to have the machine repaired. You will of course have to contact the manufacturers for this.

We trust that this now clears up the matter to your satisfaction.

Yours sincerely

- They will ignore your letter altogether.

If you receive a response like the letter you may have to consider giving up altogether which would be a pity. If you do decide to be bold it is time to present the seller with an ultimatum by inviting him to adopt a particular course of action such as giving you a refund; failing that, you will take the matter further. This is the sort of letter Mrs Sharp might write in response to the letter fobbing her off with the 'manufacturer's guarantee' excuse:

Dear Sir   [*Date*]

Thank you for your letter of [*date*] advising me to take up the matter of my defective tumble drier with the manufacturers under the terms of the guarantee. I must again remind you that it is your legal obligation under the Sale of Goods Act 1979 to remove the machine from my home, and to refund the purchase price of £215.95.

Yours faithfully

If your first letter of complaint is totally ignored, send another, again keeping a copy. You should reiterate your complaints, but this time tell the shop that if you don't get satisfaction within fourteen days you will commence legal proceedings in the County Court[1] (see overleaf). If they still don't reply it is just possible that they have done a disappearing act or ceased trading.

What if the business has disappeared or ceased trading?

If you write or return to the shop or business who sold you unsatisfactory goods to complain, only to discover that the premises are empty, it is likely that one of two things will have happened. Either the firm will simply have changed its place of business, or will have ceased trading, perhaps due to bankruptcy.

Tracing a missing business

If the business you are trying to find is a registered company, the Companies Registration Office will have particulars about it including its registered office, the official address for any correspondence. Alternatively, the Citizens Advice Bureau may help you find it. It or the Trading Standards Department[2] may have heard of other people in a similar predicament and may know some other way of assisting. It's worth a try.

If the firm has Ltd or PLC after its name it will usually be a registered company. If it is not a registered company it will either be a partnership or owned by a sole trader. Either way if the name of the firm doesn't include the names of the people running it, it may have been registered at the Business Names Registry before this was abolished in 1982.[3] Try asking traders next door or nearby if they know what has happened to the business. You could also ask to examine the rate books or the electoral register at the council offices.[4]

What if it's gone into liquidation or ceased trading?

If a firm has gone broke, getting a refund on unsatisfactory goods they sold you is not likely to prove very successful. You can only take action against a registered company as a separate entity. You can't sue the director, share-holders or employees of the company as individuals for breach of contract since they are regarded as distinct from the company. It is almost certain that in these circumstances any claim against the company would only be partially paid and you might not receive anything at all.

If the firm you were dealing with is a partnership or owned by a sole trader you can take action against the sole trader or any one or all of the partners as individuals in order to recover whatever amount you claim you are entitled to.[5]

Make your complaint in writing, preferably on a typewriter.

Mail order

If the business you were dealing with is a mail order firm and you never hear from them again having ordered goods and sent money, in many cases there is a way you can recover your money – see page 28.

Taking legal action in the Courts

Having threatened a shop or a business with legal action you're beginning to think of the costs, of lawyers and court-room dramas, and you are starting to panic. Don't. First of all threatening to take legal action in the County Court[1] does not mean you will have to go ahead and take it. Secondly, there is a simple and relatively cheap way of doing so. Where you are claiming less than £500,[6] you can look to arbitration proceedings, the procedure for taking legal action for small claims. This is explained on page 151.

Trade associations, as an alternative to taking legal action

Although taking legal action is probably simpler and cheaper than the majority of people realise (when they are claiming £500 or less[7]), there is still a general reluctance to instigate Court proceedings.

The Office of Fair Trading has been only too aware of this reluctance and in recent years a prominent feature of its work has been to encourage various trade associations to develop Codes of Practice under its guidance. The aim of these is not only to safeguard the interests of consumers over the general quality of goods and services, but also to provide a conciliation and arbitration service as a direct alternative to the dissatisfied customer taking his case before the Courts. These associations can be a great help to those who find themselves in a lingering dispute with a member of an association. The Codes of Practice already developed affect the buying of furniture, shoes, cars and domestic electrical appliances. Most of the associations covering these type of goods can assist aggrieved consumers, perhaps by arranging for the testing of an item where appropriate.

It is obviously a big advantage to choose to buy goods from firms which you know are members of a trade association. You can tell if a trader is a member

---

Keep all the correspondence and documentation to do with your complaint clean and readily available.

A raised number denotes that the complaints procedure differs in Scotland or Northern Ireland – see the end of the chapter.

---

because one of the symbols below will be prominently displayed at his business premises. If you are unable to resolve your complaint with the trader, contact the relevant trade association, sending all the details and copies of all the correspondence. See the address section for addresses and phone numbers.

Cars
Look for one of these symbols:

Motor Agents' Association

Scottish Motor Trade Association

Society of Motor Manufacturers and Traders

Vehicle Builders' and Repairers' Association

Electrical goods

These are the names and symbols to look for:

The Association of Manufacturers of Domestic Electrical Appliances
This organisation represents most British manufacturers of domestic appliances such as washing machines, spin driers, refrigerators, toasters and electrical cookers. These are known in the trade as 'white goods'.

The Radio, Electrical and Television Retailers' Association

The Electricity Council Contact the Council if your complaint is about white goods bought from an Electricity Board showroom.[8]

Northern Ireland Electricity Service

The body in Northern Ireland equivalent to the Electricity Council (see also pages 70 and 76).

Prevention is better than cure so always think twice before buying goods and services and from whom you buy them.

Furniture

There are five large trade associations which between them represent most furniture manufacturers and retailers. You will know you are protected by a Code of Practice approved by the Office of Fair Trading if you see one of these two symbols:

National Association of Retail
Furnishers

Scottish House Furnishers'
Association

Shoes

A number of trade associations in the shoe business are covered by an approved Code of Practice. Any shoe shop covered by the Code will display this symbol:

Footwear Distributors' Federation

There is no compulsion to use a trade association to help you with your complaint, but after your own attempts to sort things out it would be sensible to make use of their services which are usually free. It is usual for an association to start by offering a conciliation service between you and the trader. If it fails to bring about a peaceful settlement and you do not wish to take advantage of the arbitration service, the investigation will not prevent you from taking legal action in the Courts. But note that if you do opt for arbitration by a trade association this is usually as an alternative to taking legal action in the Courts: you cannot normally sue the trader as well. Seek advice on the choice from the Citizens Advice Bureau, the Trading Standards Department,[2] or Consumers' Association's *Which?* Personal Service (see page 167).

COMPLAINTS ABOUT GOODS BOUGHT BY MAIL ORDER

Mail order can be a very convenient way of shopping, but despite this and other advantages, complaints and disputes arise in great volume. The main kind of complaints are that:

- the goods are faulty
- the goods don't arrive at all, perhaps because the firm has gone out of business
- there is a lengthy delay over sending the goods, during which time your money is gaining interest for the firm

What you can do

Draw your complaint to the attention of the dealers at once, asking them to rectify matters. Your legal rights when buying goods by mail order are the same as those when buying from a shop. They must be as described, fit for the purpose and of merchantable quality. Before returning the goods, send the firm a letter by recorded delivery describing the defect, saying that you will be returning the goods within the next few days and that you would like the postage reimbursed. Say what you would like them to do about it. Send the goods back, also by recorded delivery, having packed them carefully. By writing this preliminary letter you will have covered yourself in case the dealers try to claim that the defect was caused when you sent the goods back.

If the firm you are dealing with is one of those that do their business exclusively through fat, glossy catalogues, then in the event of an unresolved complaint you could contact the Mail Order Traders' Association which has special procedures for dealing with complaints made against its members.

Let's suppose, though, that instead of doing your mail order business through one of these catalogues you order the goods directly in response to an advertisement in a newspaper or journal. If you have an unresolved complaint, such as the goods not arriving after you've sent your money, you should write to the advertising manager at the publication in which the advertisement appeared. Tell him:

- the date the advertisement appeared
- the name and address of the company
- the goods ordered, type, price etc
- the amount of money sent and the date

The advertising manager or one of his colleagues will then investigate your complaint. If he discovers that the firm has ceased trading or has gone into liquidation, and if the publication carrying the advertisement is a member of one of the Mail Order Protection Schemes, you should be able to get a refund from a central fund administered by the appropriate association. These schemes are run by:

- the Newspaper Publishers' Association – represents the national dailies, and the Sunday papers
- the Periodical Publishers' Association – represents most of the magazines and periodical publishers
- the Newspaper Society – represents most regional and local newspapers
- the Scottish Daily Newspapers' Society and Scottish Newspaper Proprietors' Association – represents daily and weekly newspapers respectively in Scotland

If you want to claim under any one of these schemes do so within a reasonable time and in any event within two months of your order if the advertisement was in a magazine, or within three months of the date when the newspaper carried the advertisement. It is doubtful that your claim will be met if you apply after this. A word of warning – there are some limitations to these schemes:

- they do not apply to goods ordered from a catalogue, itself obtained by response to an advertisement
- they do not apply to goods ordered through classified advertisements
- they only work when the business has ceased trading, or has gone into liquidation, and not simply when the firm is inefficient, dilatory or downright dishonest

If you can't use the schemes perhaps because one of these categories applies, you could try taking the matter up with the Advertising Standards Authority. The ASA may investigate the matter on your behalf and see that some action is taken against the firm until it meets its commitments to you and other customers. More details about the ASA can be found on page 143.

COMPLAINTS ABOUT UNSOLICITED GOODS

Imagine that out of the blue one morning the postman drops a parcel through your letterbox. You open it to discover a small pack of pre-recorded music cassettes which you haven't ordered, with a note telling you to pay for the goods after you've tried them or to send them back within so many days.

This is a typical example of a somewhat immoral trading practice that was extremely common during the '60s and early '70s and which still occasionally occurs. A note accompanying the goods tells the customer to pay immediately or send the goods back; if the goods are not returned within a set period (such as 14 days) the customer will become liable for payment. Demands for this payment usually follow, often with more goods and more demands.

If this happens to you, don't worry about it. The Unsolicited Goods and

29

Services Act 1971[9] makes this sales technique illegal and you do not have to pay for or return the goods at your own expense.

What should you do?
There are two options open to you if you receive goods in the way outlined:

- Do absolutely nothing to the goods, but make sure you keep them unused in a safe place. After six months they become yours. If the sender wants the goods back during this period he is entitled to them. You must not unreasonably refuse to send them back if he pays the postage, or refuse to allow him to collect the goods
  or
- Having received the goods, write to the sender (keeping a copy) giving him notice of the fact that you didn't ask for the goods to be sent and that you don't want them. If the sender has not collected the goods after thirty days they become your property. The sort of letter you should write is:

[Date]

Dear Sir,

On *[date]* I received a collection of tape cassettes from your firm which I did not order.

Your goods are available for collection upon reasonable notice from the above address. Please make the necessary arrangements.

Yours faithfully,

Ignore all demands to pay up and to send the goods back, unless the sender will pay the postage. Demands for payment are a criminal offence for which the sender can be prosecuted and fined. Having unsuccessfully demanded payment from you the sender may resort to threatening you with legal action if you don't pay up. Ignore these threats too, as they are also a criminal offence for which he can be further fined.

You should also report the whole business to the local office of the Trading Standards Department[2] at the Regional or County Council office.

COMPLAINTS ABOUT BROKEN DELIVERY APPOINTMENTS

You've just chosen a new three-piece suite and have arranged with the shop that they should deliver it on a particular afternoon. You cancel other appointments and arrangements for that afternoon, and wait and wait . . .

Broken delivery appointments are a very common cause of complaint. Apart from the inconvenience, what makes the issue especially frustrating is that in most cases there is very little you can do about it, other than to insist that the goods are delivered as soon as possible.

The only way to give yourself any rights in this situation is to **make time of the essence**. You should specify when you make the initial contract to buy the goods exactly when they should be delivered. Wherever possible write this date on your receipt or order form. If this time or date is broken you have the right to cancel the contract and claim back anything you've already paid.

Even if you've not made time of the essence at the outset, you are not expected by the law to wait for ever until the goods are delivered. Write to the shop or dealers straight away informing them that unless they make delivery within a specified period of time you will cancel the contract.

COMPLAINTS ABOUT FOOD

'Waiter, waiter, there's a dead fly in my soup.'
'I'm sorry, sir, I'll go and get you a live one.'

An old joke that's not very funny. It's even less funny when it becomes reality and you actually discover a foreign body in food you have bought. You are of course entitled to complain and ask for your money back as the goods are not considered to be of merchantable quality. However complaining that food is not up to standard is a potentially more serious business than simply asking for your money back.

The criminal law requires that food and drink, wherever it is sold or manufactured, must conform to certain standards. It also requires that the preparation and sale of food and drink take place in an environment that comes up to specific standards of hygiene. For example those preparing food should not smoke at the time, and suitable washing facilities should be provided and adequately maintained. This is set out in the Food and Drugs Act 1955.[10]

If you have any complaint about the quality of food you have bought or the way in which it is sold or prepared, as a matter of urgency you should inform the Environmental Health Officer at the local council offices.

COMPLAINTS ABOUT DANGEROUS GOODS

Perhaps a teddy bear has a wire sticking out of it, or an electric heater is sold without a fixed fire-guard.

If you want to complain that goods you've bought, hired or simply seen for sale are dangerous, the complaint should be made to your local Trading Standards Department[2]. The address and phone number will be listed in the telephone directory under the local authority section. The TSD will establish whether or not the item is unlawful under the Consumer Safety Act 1978 which lays down regulations about standards of safety in certain goods. The authority has the power to issue an order to a trader stopping him selling a particular item and in the most serious cases the trader can be prosecuted for being in breach of his statutory obligations.

If you have been injured by the item concerned you may also be awarded compensation upon the conviction of the trader. If you're not awarded compensation at that time, or if no prosecution is brought, you can still sue the supplier of the goods in the civil courts for breach of contract if you believe the goods are not of merchantable quality, or for negligence if the item has caused injury. In the latter case you should seek the advice of a solicitor.

Notes: Scotland and Northern Ireland

1 The Sheriff Court is the Scottish equivalent of the County Court.

2 In Northern Ireland the equivalent of the Trading Standards Department is the Trading Standards Branch of the Department of Economic Development for Northern Ireland.

3 The Business Names Registry was not abolished in Northern Ireland, and can be found at the Companies Registration Office in Belfast.

4 In Northern Ireland the electoral register will be found more commonly at the local electoral office.

5 In Scotland, as well as being able to take action against the sole trader or any or all of the partners as individuals, you can sue the partnership as a separate entity.

6 You can look to arbitration proceedings in Northern Ireland where the figure you are claiming is less than £300.

In Scotland, there is a scheme for small claims up to £1,000, known as Summary Cause, in the Sheriff Court (see page 161).

7 See above for the different maximum sums you can claim in Northern Ireland and Scotland.

8 Complaints about white goods bought at electricity board showrooms in Scotland should be addressed to the appropriate Consultative Council (see page 70) if you are unable to obtain satisfaction first from the Electricity Board concerned.

9 In Northern Ireland selling unsolicited goods is illegal under the Unsolicited Goods and Services (Northern Ireland) Order 1976.

10 The Food and Drugs (Scotland) Act 1956 and the Food and Drugs (Northern Ireland) Act 1958 apply in those countries.

Complaints about services

Calling in a plumber, having your hair cut, travelling on a bus, eating in a restaurant, going on holiday – all are examples of contracts of services, the significant word being **contract**.

If a dispute arises between you and the person providing the service, it is the contract between you both that you must first look to for guidance in the resolution of your differences. Very simply, it is the contract which dictates the obligations you owe each other. In this section we will be examining some of the basic and general legal rules involved in paying for services, and the way in which you can attempt to resolve complaints about specific services, such as the plumber who makes your pipes leak, the TV repair man who converts your colour set into a black and white one, and your luxury package holiday in the sun which turns out to be a disaster.

DISPUTES OVER PRICE, TIME AND STANDARD OF WORK

Almost all complaints about services tend to revolve round one of the following:

- the price
- the time factor
- the standard of the service provided

The price

Having shivered your way through the winter in your new home you decide to have two new central heating radiators installed. You ask Heat-It Ltd, central heating engineers, to call and give you a price for the job. The engineer calls, measures up and leaves. Two days later you get a letter from Heat-It Ltd announcing that their price will be £175. You are satisfied and tell Heat-It Ltd to get on with the job. Shortly after the work is completed you get a shock. The bill from Heat-It Ltd arrives demanding £275. When you query the bill, Heat-It Ltd reply that the engineer who called originally made a mistake and that £275 is the correct price.

This sort of dispute is typical: the person or firm providing a service demands more than the customer has anticipated. Must you pay up the extra £100?

The answer to this, and indeed to most disputes, is that you only have to pay what you **agreed** to pay, namely £175. This figure formed an important part of your contract with Heat-It Ltd, and the firm must adhere to the contract. In this situation, if either party is to suffer any loss, it must clearly be the central heating engineers.

However, when a price is given, it may be either an **estimate** or a **quote**. If it is merely an estimate the customer can expect it to vary to some degree. Heat-It Ltd might have said: 'We can't tell exactly how much the job will be at this stage but it should be around £175.' The problem, however, tends to be how much can it vary? There are no hard and fast rules on this. The law simply states that the variation must be **reasonable**.

If the price given is a quote, those providing the service cannot charge a penny more unless the customer agrees.

Another common dispute over price arises where no figure at all has been agreed on beforehand. You call the plumber out in an emergency to fix your burst pipe, or your car breaks down and you push it to the nearest garage. In both cases you simply say 'get on with the job', and no price is mentioned at this stage. If you think the eventual price is excessive, must you simply pay up whatever they ask? The answer is **no**. The Supply of Goods and Services Act 1982[3] says that if no price has been agreed on, the price charged must be reasonable. As you can imagine, determining what is reasonable can in itself be the main subject of a dispute, but if such circumstances arise there are a number of steps you can take.

- Write to the person supplying the service informing him that you regard his price as unreasonable, and that you are taking steps to discover what is a reasonable price which is the figure you will pay.
- Check with others providing a similar service in the area to determine what they might have charged, and then pay the average.
- Contact an appropriate trade association to see what they would have considered a reasonable charge and pay that.

In the extremely unlikely event that the dispute is not resolved in any of these ways and legal action is taken, it would be for the Court to determine a reasonable price (see page 151 for how to take the case to Court). If there was an obvious mathematical error, the Court may rectify it: eg when five per cent discount has been worked out as one fifth instead of one twentieth.

Note that if the trader believes the charges to be fair he has the right to retain your goods until you have paid him or until the dispute is resolved.

General tips for disputes over prices

- Always ask for the price in writing before the job is started. If someone calls to give you a price orally ask them to confirm in writing.

- If you are in doubt about whether the price given is an estimate or a quote, don't be afraid to ask, and then get the person to write which it is on your document. (But if you accept a quoted price you have to pay it even though it may turn out to be excessive or unreasonable.)
- Don't pay for someone else's mistake as in the radiators example.
- Don't be afraid to make a fuss.

The time

Imagine you're having your car repaired. You want it ready for a specific date and you make this date known to the repairer. What happens if the car is not ready in time?

The rules of the game for resolving these disputes are very similar to the ones to do with price problems. If the people providing the service have agreed on a time, then that is part of the contract and they should adhere to it. If no time is agreed, according to the Supply of Goods and Services Act 1982[3] the job must be done within a reasonable time. Again, you can check with other traders or an appropriate trade association on what would be their interpretation of a reasonable time in the circumstances.

If the people providing the service go over the time limit, when time has specifically been made of the essence, you can make them responsible for any reasonable costs the delay involves. Taking the car repair example, you would be able to hire another car and charge this to the first garage.

Standard of work

As far as disputes over standards of the service are concerned, all the same rules apply. Again, the Supply of Goods and Services Act 1982[3] says that you are entitled to services of a 'reasonable' standard. If you are in dispute with a firm over this, then again your best course of action is to check with other reputable dealers in your area providing a similar service in order to determine what is reasonable, or refer the matter to an appropriate trade association.

Exclusion clauses

It is very common in business contracts, particularly contracts for services, to find terms which attempt to exclude or limit liability for a variety of things, such as loss, damage, injury, breach of contract and so on. For instance a car parking ticket might try to claim that:

Vehicles and their contents are left at the owner's risk. No responsibility is accepted for any loss or damage to vehicles and their contents or for death or injury to persons, however caused.

These are commonly called **exclusion** or **exemption clauses**.

Over the years as clauses of this type have become more widely used and have attempted to exclude liability for a greater variety of things, more and more disputes have arisen involving them. Imagine that you go to a disco or a nightclub one evening, pay 10p for a cloakroom ticket and leave your coat. How would you react not only to the fact that it gets damaged or stolen, but that you are told you cannot get any compensation by virtue of a notice on the wall stating:

In no circumstances will the Management accept any responsibility for loss, damage or theft of a customer's property, howsoever caused.

In recent years legislation in the form of the Unfair Contract Terms Act 1977 has drastically reduced the effectiveness of these clauses, and has gone some way to restoring a balance between consumer and trader. The general position is now as follows:

- **Death or injury** Any clause which attempts to exclude liability for death or injury arising from negligence on the part of the person providing the service is of no legal effect at all.
- **Loss or damage to goods** Any clause which attempts to exclude liability for loss or damage resulting from negligence on the part of the person providing the service is also of no legal effect, unless that person can show that such a clause is fair and reasonable in the circumstances. This clause would make it almost certain that you would be able to get compensation for your lost or damaged coat in the example earlier, despite the notice on the wall, provided it was caused by the nightclub's negligence.
- **Breach of contract** Any clause which is put into one party's standard terms of business and attempts to exclude liability for breach of contract will not be valid unless it can be shown to be fair and reasonable in all the circumstances.

For example, package holiday tour operators were notorious before the Unfair Contract Terms Act 1977 for packing their booking conditions with exclusion clauses. If they changed your hotel or generally offered you a different service from that which you had originally envisaged, they were usually able to wriggle out of any responsibility by virtue of some exclusion clause. Not so now. Unless the clause is fair and reasonable (taking into account all the relevant circumstances), the company will be unable to escape its legal and moral responsibilities.

Knowledge of this Act will be an invaluable weapon in any complaint or dispute involving an exclusion clause. If such a clause is being used against you write to the manager of the firm or organisation you are in dispute with, pointing out that unless they can demonstrate to the court that their exclusion clause was fair and reasonable in all the circumstances, then under the Unfair Contract Terms Act 1977 the clause is of no legal effect whatsoever.

COMPLAINTS ABOUT TRADESMEN

Following the old adage that prevention is better than cure you should take certain precautions before employing a tradesman – whether plasterer, decorator, plumber, electrician, house builder – to provide the service you want. As we have seen, most complaints tend to arise out of arguments over the price, time, and standard of work. As far as price and time are concerned, you can go some of the way to avoiding complaints if you agree to the price in writing and by making time of the essence before any work is begun. When it comes to the standard of work, all you can do is to make sure that the person you are employing is honest, reputable and genuinely skilled in the trade he professes to practise. In other words, if you answer an advertisement written on a postcard in a newsagent's window, and the advertiser tells you he can build your house extension in half the time and for half the price of any other builder, you have only yourself to blame if you accept and things begin to go wrong.

One way to be reasonably sure of your choice of builder or other tradesman is to make sure that he is a member of an appropriate trade association. While this is of course no positive guarantee against trouble, it is unlikely that a firm of 'botch-up merchants' will be members. Furthermore, if things do go wrong and you find yourself with a complaint, you can turn to the trade association – they often assist consumers with complaints against member firms. Ask the business concerned to confirm in writing that it is a member of a trade association, and if you are still in doubt, check with the trade association itself.

Builders

If you are buying a new house, or having a house built, make sure that the builder is on the register of the National House Building Council (NHBC) and that the house is covered by the NHBC's protection scheme. The way it works is this. The NHBC will monitor the progress on houses being built by their registered builders by making regular inspections. When the house is finished, if the NHBC inspector is satisfied that the builder has conformed to the Council's standards, he will issue a **Ten Year Protection Certificate** now known as **Notice of Insurance Cover**. The effect of this protection is that:

- During the first two years the builder must put right, at his own expense, any defects which may arise as a result of his failure to comply with the NHBC's minimum standards.
- During the next eight years the NHBC will provide cover against any major structural damage brought about because of the failure of the builder to comply with the Council's standards.
- The NHBC will also provide cover against the builder's bankruptcy or liquidation.

It is important to note that if your house is covered by the NHBC protection scheme, you should draw to the attention of the builder any defects in the property as soon as practicable after they become apparent. Failure to do so may jeopardise your chances of claiming successfully under the NHBC scheme.

If a complaint arises about a claim under the scheme, for example if a builder refuses to honour his obligations under the cover provided, the NHBC runs a special conciliation and arbitration service to resolve such complaints. Its booklet *Disputes about Defects – Notes for Purchasers and Vendors* is available free and provides a comprehensive and well-written guide about the procedure.

Unfortunately, of course, the scheme only applies when a registered builder builds a new house; it does not apply to repairs or alteration work, nor, of course, to those builders who are not registered with the NHBC.

If you have a complaint about a builder or building work not covered by the NHBC scheme, all you can do is to fall back on your basic contractual rights looked at earlier in this section and take appropriate legal action. Another trade association to which a reputable builder may belong is the National Federation of Building Trades Employers.

Plumbers

If you require advice over some technical plumbing matter involved in a complaint, such as what constitutes a reasonable standard of work, the Institute of Plumbing can help.

Electricians

The Electrical Contractors' Association (ECA) and the Electrical Contractors Association of Scotland both operate schemes providing a guarantee of minimum standards of work among their members and will deal with complaints about those members. The National Inspection Council for Electrical Installation Contractors (NICEIC) also maintains a register of approved contractors.

Gas men   (not those employed by British Gas: see page 71)

The Confederation for the Registration of Gas Installers (CORGI) is responsible for maintaining a register of gas installers whose standards are regularly monitored so that they comply with all the gas safety regulations. CORGI can also deal with complaints against members.[4]

Complain as soon as possible. A delay may weaken your argument.

Decorators

The British Decorators' Association operates a complaints service for work done by members. Where the standard of work is in dispute, it can supply an inspection service and a written report which a complainant could use as evidence in Court, should a complaint get that far.

Complaints about servicing and repairs

Imagine you take your car into the local garage for its 30,000 mile service. When you return to collect the car you are dubious that it has even been examined because the same mysterious clanking noise is there. Furthermore, you are presented with an almighty bill for spare parts. What can you do?

In this sort of case, and indeed in any case involving servicing or repair work, you must:

- Make your complaint known to the dealer as soon as it arises, and tell him what you expect him to do about it.
- Write to the dealer formally outlining your complaint if complaining in person gets no results.

- It will add substantially to the weight of any such letter if you can enclose a condemnation of the work that was done, supplied either by another (reputable) dealer or an organisation such as the RAC or AA in the case of disputes over motor car repairs and servicing.
- You could discover whether or not the dealer belongs to an appropriate trade association and refer the matter to it, asking for an investigation.
- If all else fails you could revert to your basic legal rights and sue, using the procedures outlined on page 151. Ultimately, the dispute is about whether or not the work was done to a reasonable standard.

Broken appointments

If a repair man has undertaken to call at a certain time and doesn't turn up or is substantially late, he has broken part of his contract and you are entitled to compensation. Deduct a reasonable sum from the bill and send a letter explaining why you have paid less than asked. You can claim for telephone calls to find out what is going on and for additional expenses such as using a launderette for your washing if it is your washing machine that needs repairing.

If you've taken time off work and they know this, you can claim for loss of earnings too. At any rate claim something like ten per cent of the bill for wasted time and inconvenience. If everyone did this repair men might become a bit more punctual.

COMPLAINTS ABOUT BUSES

How you handle your complaint depends on which company's bus you are complaining about.[5]

Local authority buses

If the bus or service you wish to complain about is operated by your local authority, you will have quite a job trying to penetrate the bureaucratic wall surrounding the organisation and the services it offers.

The matter should only be dealt with formally in writing – an oral complaint will get you absolutely nowhere. Your first letter should go to the local authority's transport manager. If that doesn't get a satisfactory result, write to the Chairman of the Transport Committee. You can always complain to your local councillors if that fails too.

One point, however, if you set out on a trail of vengeance against such a local service – make sure that it is worth it, both in terms of what you and the rest of the public will get out of it. Don't waste the time of the people you are complaining to with a trivial matter that simply prevents them performing the very service you expect of them.

The largest local authority bus service in the country is London Transport, which is also responsible for the Underground. If you have a complaint of any type against it, these are the people (in order of priority) your letter(s) should be addressed to:

- the Public Relations Officer
- the Chairman of London Transport Passengers' Committee
- the Chairman of London Transport

Nationwide bus companies

The National Bus Company, based in London, is parent to thirty subsidiary companies dotted around the country so the first step is to contact the appropriate person within that particular company. Only when you fail to get any satisfaction should you write to the General Manager. As before, your only chance of registering an effective complaint is to put it in writing as soon as the subject of the complaint arises.

If your complaint involves some aspect of the overall operation of the **National Express** long distance coach service, write to the Service Standards Manager of the company.

The General Manager is the complaints contact at **National Holidays**.

If you are dissatisfied with the outcome, considerable additional pressure might be put on the company from outside:

- Contact your local authority's Transport Department and ask them to look into the matter (the National Bus Company derives a small part of its revenue from local authorities).
- Make your complaint to the Regional Traffic Commissioner. The Traffic Commissioners exercise a general supervisory role over the standards of bus operations, and it is they who are responsible for licensing operators' vehicles and services.
- Ask your solicitor or Citizens Advice Bureau if you want to take legal action with a view to getting compensation.

COMPLAINTS ABOUT BRITISH RAIL

The timekeeping of trains, the quality of train and station services, passenger information, conduct of staff, overcrowding in carriages, high fares and expensive snacks – these are some of the most common areas of complaint made against British Rail.[6]

When you travel with British Rail you enter into a contract. You agree to pay the fare and they agree to get you to your destination in one piece. Simple enough, you might think, but the problem occurs when you realise that their obligation to get you to your destination is taken quite literally as that, and

41

nothing more. The fact that you arrive three hours late and miss your job interview, feeling exhausted and ill from having to stand up the whole time because there were no seats, is in no way breach of contract.

If you are generally dissatisfied with British Rail's services, write to the Divisional Manager in the appropriate British Rail Region, explaining the nature of your dissatisfaction and suggesting what you would like to be done about the situation.

If your complaint involves an issue of general policy, or if you are not satisfied with the way it has been dealt with at regional level, write to the Chairman of British Rail at the Board's London headquarters.

If you are still not satisfied after taking these steps, write to your area secretary of the Transport Users' Consultative Committee or the Northern Irish equivalent (look them up in the phone book) whose job is to help people with complaints about train services and other facilities provided by British Rail.

At national level the Central Transport Consultative Committee, of which the Chairmen of the Area Committees are members, co-ordinates the work of the area Committees.

Don't hesitate to write to these organisations. If it is possible to help you with any justified complaint, they will do so.

COMPLAINTS ABOUT AIR TRAVEL

Here are a few useful tips and points of information about the most common problems that give customers cause to complain about air travel services.

Delays

If a delay has been caused by a strike, weather conditions or something outside the control of the airline, there's nothing you can do.

If a delay is caused by something the airline could have avoided, it must pay you compensation for any loss you have suffered – for example, the cost of staying overnight in a hotel near the airport, or for additional meals. You can't claim compensation for losses which you couldn't have expected the airline to know about, such as failure to win a contract through missing an important business meeting. Also note that most airlines are party to the Carriage by Air and Road Act 1979 under which there are certain statutory limits for compensation.

However, in many cases airlines will not even need to be asked but will simply offer accommodation and compensation to delayed passengers. If they don't, ask the airline's duty officer at the airport and if this proves unsuccessful, take the matter up later with the airline's Customer Relations Officer, and ultimately the Chief Executive. But airlines are very conscious of their public image and it is unlikely that you will need to go that far.

Overbooking

It is a sad fact of commercial life that some airlines deliberately overfill their flights. In doing so they are assuming through experience that several would-be passengers will cancel for one reason or another, leaving a neat fully-booked flight. If you can't get a seat on the flight you booked, the airline is in breach of contract and may have to pay you compensation for whatever loss you have suffered, provided it is one that could reasonably have been foreseen.

The major airlines sometimes offer special compensation arrangements to passengers who cannot get a seat because of overbooking. These usually amount to an offer of a guarantee to get the passengers to their destination within so many hours, or to pay compensation. If you accept this deal, however, you will probably have to give up any rights to further legal action, but given the old saying 'a bird in the hand . . .' the deal is worth accepting.

Luggage

You fly home from foreign parts, wishing you could have stayed away longer, only to discover that your luggage has done just that or has even gone on a world tour without you. If your luggage is lost, at the moment the compensation you can claim from the airline is the sterling equivalent of $20 per kilogram. If you are carrying something of particular value which leads you to feel that compensation at this level is going to leave you short, your answer is to take out adequate insurance cover beforehand, or you can pay an 'excess value charge' at the check-in desk to cover valuable items. If you find that your luggage is damaged, complain in writing as soon as you discover it. A delay may ruin your chances of being able to claim.

Taking your complaint further

Airlines, as we said, are anxious to keep their customers happy, so it is unlikely that they will prove unreasonable to your demands arising out of a justified complaint. But if you still feel you have had a raw deal, contact the Air Transport Users' Committee (AUC), whose function is to further the interests of air transport users generally. (Complaints about hotel accommodation and other facilities incorporated as part of a package tour are outside the scope of the AUC and should be referred to the Association of British Travel Agents.)

AUC is interested to hear of complaints about suppliers of air transport, whether airline, travel agent, tour operator or air-freight shipper. You should send full written details and enclose copies of any relevant letters or documents. The complaint will then be forwarded to the courier or travel organisation concerned under a covering letter setting out the main features for investigation and comment.

The complaint is also circulated for information, when appropriate, to the Board of Airline Representatives in the UK (BARUK), the International Air Transport Association (IATA), the Association of British Travel Agents (ABTA), and the Civil Aviation Authority UK (CAA). In this way a certain amount of pressure from within the industry can be put on airlines and couriers where justified. As a testimonial to the Air Transport Users' Committee, recent figures show that in 41 per cent of complaints that have been channelled through them, financial compensation or an acceptable explanation has been achieved for the complainants.

COMPLAINTS ABOUT PACKAGE HOLIDAYS

Glossy holiday brochures are full of romantic images and promises of fair play and administrative efficiency. But every year thousands of those images are destroyed by a disappointing and even distressing holiday which has to be endured for the entire period of the booking.

Holidays are meant to be enjoyed but enjoyment is an extremely subjective concept. A noisy sleepless night to one person will be a lively night out in the hotel disco to someone else. Similarly, a nice quiet hotel to some customers will be deadly boring to another. The same can be said of most of the facilities provided by a typical tour operator. It all depends on your own personal tastes, and most importantly, **your expectations**.

On package holidays, like many other things, you tend to get what you pay for. So be realistic: if you go on a two-week package to Spain at the height of the season, at an all-inclusive price of £147 for full board at Hotel Drizzle, then despite the marketing techniques used in the brochure, which is after all designed to sell, you can only expect the food, service and facilities to reflect the price.

Most genuine complaints that win compensation are based on breach of contract. When you book up to go on a package holiday, you make a contract with the tour operator (**not** the travel agent who simply arranges your booking). If the tour operator fails to supply you with the service he has promised, he is in breach of contract and is under a legal obligation to offer you some sort of remedy (but watch out for exclusion clauses in the booking conditions).

Incidentally, most disputes between a dissatisfied holidaymaker and a tour operator tend to be not over obtaining compensation itself but over the amount. Tour operators are generally very willing to send an apologetic letter to a dissatisfied customer and will normally extend a very small ex gratia payment without admitting liability, or offer a discount on your next holiday with that firm. However, when it comes to pressing them for genuine compensation they tend to dig their heels in, and it can take a great deal of time, patience, know-how and sometimes even money to extract their heels from their deeply entrenched positions.

With these points in mind, let's examine exactly what course of action you might follow to obtain the best results when you have a genuine and justified complaint.

- **Make your complaint known to the tour operator's representative on the spot.** Most reputable tour operators have on-the-spot representatives who make themselves available at frequent intervals throughout your stay. Look at some of the things the brochures say.

    RESORT REPRESENTATIVES
    In each of our resorts we have Resident Representatives whose sole task is to help you get the best out of your holiday and ensure that all aspects of it operate as smoothly as possible. It is their task to eliminate irritations unobtrusively and to ensure that your hotel reception runs smoothly.

    Unfortunately, all too often these representatives appear to have little if any influence and if this appears to be the case, proceed to the next stage.

- **Go to see the area manager** Many tour operators have an office in popular holiday areas where an area manager may be present. This person will usually have more authority than the hotel representative. He may even be the mysterious superior which the hotel representative promised he had been consulting over your complaint.

- **Put your complaint in writing** The tour operator has you at a distinct disadvantage. You have already paid. You are thousands of miles from home. Whatever he offers you in response to your complaints, you are more than likely, despite your very loud protests, to accept in the hope that you can successfully take up the matter when you get home. In short, you decide for the time being to make the best of a bad job. But you can also at this stage send a letter to the company at its head office, giving brief details of what has happened, and saying that for the present you have no choice but to accept things, but that you reserve all rights when you get home to take action against it for breach of contract. This way the company cannot argue that you accepted whatever solution was offered as a full settlement of your dispute.
- **Complain on arrival home** When you get home take up the matter immediately by writing to the company, this time outlining your complaint in detail and saying exactly what you want it to do about it. If you want compensation, say how much. Refer to what other people on the trip thought: you might try to get something in writing from them before you part your ways. Send the package operator a copy of your letter.

  The likely response will be an apologetic letter, perhaps offering a discount on your next holiday with the company, or a small ex gratia payment without admitting any liability, purely as a gesture of good will. If you wish to reject the offer because the company's failure to live up to its pre-trip promises has substantially impaired the enjoyment of your holiday, you should seek help and advice.
- **Seek help and advice** Most of the correspondence going backwards and forwards (and be assured there will be plenty of it) will revolve around legal arguments. The Citizens Advice Bureau or Trading Standards Department[2] will always offer free advice. Make the most of it. If you believe that the company is in breach of contract you can always take legal action in the County Court[1] using the procedure described on page 151, but don't use the threat of this until all else has failed.
- **Association of British Travel Agents – ABTA** Before taking legal action, one other place you should go to for help is the Association of British Travel Agents, so long as the package company is a member. The Association represents most large tour operators and reputable travel agents and, with the assistance of the Office of Fair Trading, has drawn up a Code of Practice to help improve standards, to which all its members should adhere.

Some disputes involve a lengthy correspondence. Don't start unless you have got the patience and the stomach to see it through.

This sign on brochures and letterheads tells customers which firms are members. If you wish ABTA will attempt to resolve your complaint by conciliation with the firm concerned. If the conciliation procedure fails, ABTA will offer you the opportunity of referring the dispute for arbitration by the Institute of Arbitrators. This can only take place within nine months of the holiday. It is a direct alternative to taking legal action: you can't do both, so you should take advice.

Brochure descriptions

If your complaint is that the brochure description does not correspond with what you discover to be reality, the holiday company may be in breach of the Trade Descriptions Act 1968. Your local Trading Standards Department[2] (under the Local Authority Section in the phone book) is responsible for enforcement of this Act. The Criminal Courts have powers to award compensation to victims in certain circumstances.

COMPLAINTS AGAINST RESTAURANTS

Eating out ought to be a pleasurable experience, but if the food and service don't live up to what you would hope for, here are a few useful tips:

- Complain immediately. Too many people eat their meal muttering about the restaurant and don't complain at all, or only complain that the food was off after they have eaten it. If you think there is something wrong, complain immediately, when there is the maximum opportunity of doing something about it.
- When you eat out, whether in a café, restaurant or pub, you enter into a contract with those providing the service. Under the contract the standard of service and food provided must be reasonable. What is reasonable will depend on many factors, such as the type of establishment and the price being paid.
- Your complaint should first be made to the waiter serving you. If the food is unacceptable, reject it straight away. The restaurant will usually rectify the problem immediately, thus avoiding any unpleasantness.

- Only when the waiter is unable or unwilling to put things right should you complain to the manager. Do so in a polite but firm way and try not to lose your temper.

- As a final step if you have failed through reasonable discussion to sort things out satisfactorily, you could consider making a deduction from the bill. You do not have to pay for food which falls below the required standard: you can simply deduct a reasonable sum, giving details of why, and provide your name and address. The same applies if you regard the standard of service as unreasonable, for example if you have been kept waiting nearly an hour before being served or between courses. This is fairly drastic action, and should be avoided wherever possible. Alternatively, you could pay up making it clear that you're doing so 'without prejudice to my legal rights'. You would then have to sue to get your money, or part of it, back. You don't need to leave a tip if the service is seriously deficient.

- In particularly serious cases the criminal law exercises some degree of influence over restaurant management. If you feel that the food is not fit for human consumption, or if you have reason to believe that food is being prepared in unhygienic conditions, report the matter to the local authority (Environmental Health Officer) who will investigate your complaint and who might prosecute the offender under appropriate legislation. You may be compensated if affected.

- Don't be afraid to complain. Remember that it is only by doing so that standards will ultimately improve.

Notes: Scotland and Northern Ireland

1 The Sheriff Court is the Scottish equivalent of the County Court.

2 In Northern Ireland the equivalent of the Trading Standards Department is the Trading Standards Branch of the Department of Economic Development for Northern Ireland.

3 In Scotland the Supply of Goods and Services Act does not apply, but Scots common law is broadly similar.

4 Neither British Gas nor CORGI operates in Northern Ireland. Where gas is available it is supplied on a Town Gas basis and enquiries and complaints should be directed to the office of the local gas company.

5 The Scottish Transport Group, based in Edinburgh, is the parent body which covers the Scottish Bus Group. SBG consists of seven subsidiaries. Complaints should be made to the general manager of the particular subsidiary, and only as a last resort to the chairman of the SBG. Scottish City Link is the trading title of the long distance coach service run by the SBG.

   There are two public bus undertakings in Northern Ireland: Ulsterbus (Rural Service) and Citybus (Belfast Service). Mr Werner Heubeck is the managing director of both undertakings and complaints should be addressed to him or to the Northern Ireland Transport Users Committee.

6 British Rail operates the Larne–Stranraer car ferry but does not otherwise operate in Northern Ireland. The principal public rail undertaking is Northern Ireland Railways to which complaints (addressed to the manager) should be directed.

Complaints about the professions

COMPLAINTS ABOUT THE LEGAL PROFESSION

The two branches of the legal profession – solicitors and barristers – have separate governing bodies and thus separate complaints procedures.

Solicitors

The first step to take if you think your solicitor is guilty of **professional misconduct** is to complain to him face to face. What you think is a matter for complaint and grievance may in fact have a perfectly reasonable and satisfactory explanation. For example you may believe the solicitor is being slow when in fact he is waiting for a reply to a letter he has sent on your behalf. The majority of complaints arise not because of incompetence or lack of interest but through both parties failing to communicate with each other. Both solicitor and client should keep in touch, the solicitor to let the client know what is happening, and the client to jog the solicitor's memory. Don't be afraid to ring your solicitor to ask how things are progressing, but don't pester him unnecessarily.

If the grievance isn't settled with the solicitor himself, write to his senior partner, either giving details of your complaint or asking for an appointment to discuss the grievance. The senior partner may ask the solicitor in question to give an explanation and rectify matters if appropriate.

Complaints to the Law Society

The Law Society is the governing body of solicitors[1]. Most large towns and cities have their own independent local branches and a dispute that you can't resolve with an individual firm of solicitors can be made to the local secretary: look them up in the phone book or ask at the Citizens Advice Bureau. Their powers are limited, however – they can really only look into fairly minor complaints in an informal way – although they do exercise considerable influence over local solicitors.

Give the person or body you are complaining about a chance to voice their side of the case and to put things right first. This will probably save everyone a lot of wasted time and aggravation.

If your complaint is a serious one it should be made to the headquarters of the Law Society. The Society has powers both to investigate complaints and to take action where appropriate. Where an investigation reveals that a serious breach of the Law Society's high standards of professional behaviour has occurred, the Society can try the solicitor before a disciplinary committee. This committee can fine him or even stop him from practising, but it cannot make him pay compensation to you as the victim of the complaint.

The Law Society will deal with the following matters, all classed as **professional misconduct**:

- persistent delay in answering letters
- not accounting to you for money held on your behalf
- not keeping your business confidential
- acting for someone else in the same matter where your interests conflict
- taking advantage of your age or inexperience
- overcharging
- dishonesty

You should always complain about any of these breaches.

The Law Society cannot:

- give you legal advice
- recommend any solicitor by name or firm
- compel a solicitor to act for you
- tell your solicitor how to proceed with your affairs if he is acting properly
- order your solicitor to hand over your papers if you have not paid his costs
- order your solicitor to pay you compensation
- take proceedings on your behalf against your solicitor for his negligence or lack of care when doing your work
- investigate your complaint if it is about a solicitor who is acting for someone else (except in certain circumstances)

If you are satisfied that the matter is something the Law Society can deal with, write to: The Secretary, Professional Purposes, at the Society's office (for England and Wales). The address section also gives the addresses for complaints about solicitors in Scotland[2] and Northern Ireland.

Give the name and address of the solicitor you are complaining about and state briefly and concisely the basis of your complaint. Do not send any documents at this stage. Also confirm in your letter that the Law Society has your authority to send the solicitor concerned a copy of your letter for his explanation. This is a perfectly reasonable thing to do as there are of course two sides to any complaint.

Complaints that your solicitor has been negligent

Through this complaints procedure the Law Society only deals with complaints about solicitors' **misconduct**, and does not investigate allegations of

negligence.[3] It makes this very clear in the leaflet *Complaints to the Law Society about Solicitors* where it states:

> The Society's control over solicitors' behaviour is limited to their professional conduct or, in other words, to matters affecting their honour and integrity as distinct from their competence.

If you believe that negligence has occurred your remedy is to take legal action. You should discover exactly what your legal rights are in this situation by consulting another solicitor or the Citizens Advice Bureau. One problem that complainants often raise at this stage is the difficulty of finding one solicitor prepared to take another solicitor to task. The Law Society maintains a 'negligence panel' of senior solicitors who will advise in such cases.[3] What you get is an hour's free advice from one of them. Write to the Secretary, Professional Purposes, at the Society's office. It is usually not necessary to go to Court as most negligence claims are settled beforehand. It is for this reason that all solicitors have to have compulsory insurance.

Complaints about overcharging[4]

If you genuinely consider that the charges your solicitor is making for his services are unfair, this is what you can do:

- If the work did not involve Court work, or if, as the lawyers say, it was **non-contentious**, in most cases you are entitled to ask and ultimately to insist that the solicitor apply to the Law Society for what is called a **remuneration certificate**. The solicitor must tell you about the certificate before he can sue you for unpaid fees, and you must apply for one within a month of being told about it. What happens is this. All the details of the work undertaken, and the client's comments, are examined by a panel of solicitors appointed by the Law Society. They will issue a remuneration certificate which will state whether or not in the Society's opinion the bill was fair and reasonable. If they feel the bill should be reduced, the certificate will state what the charge should be. The panel has no authority to increase the bill. There is no charge made to the client.
- If the work has involved **contentious** business, in other words, if Court proceedings have been commenced, the Law Society cannot intervene in the question of costs. This is left to the Courts who will assess the bill to decide what is fair and reasonable. This process is known as **having the bill taxed**. The local Court office will advise you on the procedure to follow.

The Lay Observer[5]

If you are unhappy with the way the Law Society has handled your complaint, or perhaps dissatisfied with the decision it has taken, you can ultimately refer your dissatisfaction to the Lay Observer at the Royal Courts of Justice in

London. He will consider the Law Society's treatment of your complaint but not the merits of the complaint itself.

He will firstly ask to see the Law Society's file of correspondence dealing with the matter and will then submit a report to you, the complainant, with copies to the Law Society and the solicitor at the centre of your complaint. The Lay Observer may recommend to the Society either beforehand, or as part of the report, that they make further investigation into certain aspects of the complaint. He may also make any recommendation he considers appropriate under the circumstances.

The Lay Observer has no authority when it comes to complaints about barristers.[5]

Complaints about barristers[6]

The professional body who will investigate any complaint relating to the professional conduct of a barrister is the Bar Council, but before registering an official complaint with them it is worth writing to the barrister's Head of Chambers at the same address. He may be able to clear up a number of complaints much more informally. This still leaves you with the option of complaining formally to the Bar Council if you are unhappy with the response from the barrister's Head of Chambers. You should include the following information in the letter to the Bar Council:

- the name of the barrister concerned, and his professional address (if known)
- the name and address of the solicitors who employed the barrister on your behalf
- if your complaint relates to Court proceedings, the title or number of the Court, the names of the parties involved in the Court action and the dates of the hearing
- a detailed statement of your complaint
- names and addresses of any people who could provide the Bar Council with extra relevant information
- if the complaint relates to events which occurred more than twelve months previously, give the reason for the delay in making it

Your complaint will be referred for consideration to the Professional Conduct Committee which will usually order any investigations necessary. Often this amounts to getting comments and further information from the barrister concerned and from any other individuals. The Committee will then consider the complaint and take one of the following courses of action:

- recognise that there seems to be a case of professional misconduct and refer the matter to a Disciplinary Tribunal for a full hearing, with oral evidence and witnesses

- recognise that the barrister seems to have been in breach of professional standards. This is something that can be dealt with by the Committee itself and does not involve a full hearing
- decide that the barrister has neither been guilty of any professional misconduct nor is in breach of professional standards

As the complainant you will be advised of the Committee's decision about your complaint, but you will not be given the reasons for the decision.

Be warned that the most you are likely to get out of complaining, **if** your complaint is upheld, is the satisfaction of hearing that the barrister has been officially reprimanded. In very serious cases he might be disbarred or suspended. The point is, you will not receive any compensation at all even if this seems the most appropriate remedy. To get compensation you would have to take legal action against the barrister which might well prove fruitless as in certain circumstances, especially when the handling of the case in Court is concerned, barristers are immune from actions for negligence.

COMPLAINTS ABOUT DOCTORS (GPs)

Complaints about National Health Service general practitioners

There are two major bodies to whom you can complain about a doctor: which one you choose depends on your complaint. Both bodies exercise a different type of influence over a doctor. **The General Medical Council** supervises the entire medical profession and all doctors must belong to it in order to practise lawfully. A doctor's relationship with the GMC is therefore a purely professional one. Secondly, a National Health Service general practitioner is of course influenced by the NHS, the relationship being a contractual one. The NHS too will be interested in some complaints.

Ask yourself whether or not your complaint is a question of serious professional misconduct or one of a generally poor service provided by the doctor. If it is the former, contact the General Medical Council. What you consider to be generally poor service should be reported to your local **Family Practitioner Committee**[7] (address in the phone book). This is the NHS body that administrates GPs.

Examples of serious professional misconduct

- carrying out illegal abortions
- indecently assaulting a patient
- having an improper relationship with a patient
- being drunk while attending to a patient
- disclosing confidential information

Examples of poor service

- dirty surgery
- rudeness by a receptionist attempting to give medical advice over the phone
- rudeness by a doctor
- failure to attend a patient when asked to do so

The lists are of course not exhaustive but should give some idea of the distinction between the types of complaints. If you are not sure which category your complaint falls into, or if you think that there is some overlap, complain to the Family Practitioner Committee.

Investigation of complaints by the Family Practitioner Committee[7]

If you want to make a complaint about your doctor to the Family Practitioner Committee with whom he has his contract of service, make the complaint in writing within eight weeks[8] of the event which gave rise to the complaint. Matters raised outside this time limit may only be investigated if the FPC is satisfied that there is a reasonable cause for the delay, for example, illness. To deal with the complaint the FPC would also require either the consent of the doctor concerned or that of the Secretary of State for Social Services.

The FPC may receive complaints for investigation from:

- the patient who was, or claimed to be, entitled to the provision of the services of the practitioner
- a person who has the authority of the patient
- a person writing on behalf of the patient who is, because of old age, sickness or other infirmity, incapable of making a complaint, or on behalf of a patient who is under eighteen
- anyone complaining concerning a deceased person

Your letter will firstly be considered by the Chairman of the appropriate service committee of the FPC; in the case of doctors (as opposed to opticians, pharmacists etc.) it will be the Medical Service Committee. If the Chairman decides that there may well be some substance to the complaint he will:

- seek the observations of the doctor in question, giving him four weeks to reply
- send the doctor's reply to you for your comments which must be made within two weeks

The correspondence will then be reconsidered by the Chairman. If he is of the opinion that there is still a case for the doctor to answer:
either
- he will refer the case to the entire Service Committee for thorough investigation by way of a formal hearing (this involves the presentation of oral evidence, and the questioning of witnesses where appropriate). Representation by a member of the legal profession is not permitted
  or
- where the Chairman considers a full hearing unnecessary, he will report the case to the entire Service Committee who can decide what action should be taken against the doctor, without the need for a formal hearing

Of course on examining the correspondence the Chairman may be of the opinion that there is no real case for the doctor to answer so he will dismiss it. As the complainant you will be advised of this and asked whether you wish to take the matter further by submitting an additional statement. Alternatively, the Chairman may recommend that the doctor limit the number of patients on his list, or that he receive a warning from the Secretary of State, or that his salary be withheld.

Both parties to the complaint have a right to appeal to the Secretary of State for Social Services against a decision of the FPC.

It is also usual practice for the FPC to issue to the press a short summary of the complaint, the committee's decision, and what action has been taken. The names and details of the parties to the action are not published.

Weigh up what you have to gain by complaining.

Making a complaint to the General Medical Council

If you believe that your complaint involves serious professional misconduct on the part of a doctor, it is open to you to write to the General Medical Council who will scrutinise the complaint very carefully. Of course complaints concerning behaviour which may be regarded as serious professional misconduct reach the GMC from a number of other sources: sometimes, for example, the police will inform them if the conviction of a doctor has taken place. Furthermore, where a matter has already been investigated through some other procedure – for example by a Family Practitioner Committee – the Secretary of State reports that Committee's findings to the GMC.

Again, as a complainant you will not recover any compensation whatsoever through complaining to the GMC. You are pursuing the case through social conscience, so that if a doctor **is** guilty of serious professional misconduct his governing body may know about it. In this way it can consider what action should be taken both to protect the public from a repeated occurrence of his misconduct; and of course the GMC is also keen to protect the reputation and standards of the medical profession generally. With these aims in mind the Professional Conduct Committee will decide whether or not a doctor is guilty of serious professional misconduct and will direct what if any disciplinary action should be taken.

Where to get help and advice

In making a complaint about a doctor you will encounter a minefield of committees and very often some quite lengthy and complicated procedures. **Do not** let this put you off. If in doubt the Community Health Council[9] (under Community in the phone book; see also page 98) will give you advice and in some cases will assist you at all stages.

Taking legal action

Taking action against a doctor by invoking the procedures described may give you some personal satisfaction but it may not make up for an injury. If you feel that a doctor has acted negligently, you can sue him for negligence, claiming compensation. If this is what you have in mind, seek advice from a solicitor who specialises in medical negligence cases (ask at the Citizens Advice Bureau for a list). AVMA (Action for the Victims of Medical Accidents) may be of help, particularly if you live in the London area.

You should realise however that successfully pursuing a negligence case against a doctor is extremely difficult. You have to be able to prove not only that he was wrong in what he did, or the way he did it, but that other competent doctors would not have acted in the same way in the circumstances. In other words, you must be able to prove that he did not exercise 'reasonable care' and that he did not act as 'a reasonable doctor' would have done in the same situation. If your case is one of the few where the doctor's actions are blatantly negligent your case may be comparatively easy to prove. Examples of such negligence might be where a pregnant woman is injected with a German measles vaccine resulting in damage to the unborn child, or where a doctor fails to check your records and prescribes a drug to which you are allergic with drastic consequences. Where the negligence is debatable, as in most cases, your legal action may prove to be an expensive and lengthy procedure, with no guarantee of success.

Complaints about doctors in private practice

If your doctor treats you privately the arrangement is looked on as a contract – in other words as with anyone providing a service he must charge a reasonable amount for a reasonable job done. If you do have cause for complaint, approach the General Medical Council.

Complaints against hospital doctors and staff

This topic is dealt with separately on page 96.

COMPLAINTS ABOUT DENTISTS

The most common general causes for complaint about dentists are given below with practical suggestions for dealing with them.

Professional misconduct

If you believe that a dentist has been guilty of serious unprofessional behaviour involving misconduct, for example being drunk while giving treatment, you should complain to the **General Dental Council**, the professional body for dentists with whom they have to be registered in order to practise. Write to the Registrar of the Council giving full particulars. An investigation will be made which may ultimately lead to disciplinary action being taken against the dentist. Note that the GDC has no power to award you compensation.

Poor service

If you have a complaint that treatment or service from a dentist which you are receiving on the National Health Service is poor, for example about the appointments system or unhygienic conditions, complain to the **Family Practitioner Committee**[10] for the area in which the dentist practises (the address can be found in any post office or the telephone book). You should make the complaint within eight weeks of the matter giving rise to the complaint, or within six months of the completion of the course of treatment. The Family Practitioner Committee has an investigation procedure which may lead to some disciplinary action against the dentist. If the Committee feels that serious professional misconduct is involved it will report the matter to the

General Dental Council. Again it is important to note that the Family Practitioner Committee has no power to award any compensation. If you have a complaint about a dentist treating you privately, tell the General Dental Council.

Negligence

If your complaint is that the dentist has been negligent and you are seeking compensation you must look to the law for a remedy. Taking legal action against a professional person is never easy, and you should seek advice from a solicitor.

COMPLAINTS ABOUT OPTICIANS

If you have cause to complain about an optician, remember that it is always worth discussing the matter with your optician first.

Professional misconduct

If you want to complain that an optician's behaviour has been improper in some way, contact the **General Optical Council**, the professional body with whom all opticians have to be registered in order to practise, or the British College of Ophthalmic Opticians to which most opticians belong. For an ophthalmic medical practitioner (a doctor with qualifications in diseases of the eye and their treatment) or consulting ophthalmologist, write to the General Medical Council.

The Association of Optical Practitioners may also be able to help with such a complaint if it involves one of their members. Write to them with details; they will send a copy of your letter to the optician concerned, inviting his comments. They will then act as an arbitration service to try to bring about a conclusion that is satisfactory to both parties.

Poor service

Any complaint involving what you regard as generally poor service, for example an unreliable appointments system or the charges for National Health Service frames or lenses, should be made to the local Family Practitioner Committee.[11] Its Ophthalmic Service Committee will investigate this type of complaint, and will try to arbitrate a resolution satisfactory to both you and the optician concerned. The FPC has no power to award any compensation. You would have to take legal action if this is what you wanted (see page 151). See overleaf if your complaint concerns private frames and/or lenses.

■ If you just can't get used to wearing the NHS glasses the optician has prescribed for you and feel that they are simply not right for you, first obtain the permission of the FPC to seek another eye test with your own or a different optician. Then if it turns out that the original prescription was wrong, or that the lenses have been incorrectly made up, NHS lenses can be changed at no charge to you. This procedure is only available for about three months after the first test.

■ If you feel that you have been over-charged for your NHS glasses, first check with the optician who dispensed them. If you still want to complain, you will need a copy of your prescription from the optician to send to the FPC.

■ If you are having to wait a long time for your new glasses to arrive, all you can do is chivvy the optician.

Negligence
If you believe that wrongly prescribed glasses have caused you to be injured or suffer some loss, you may have a case for negligence. Such cases are likely to be lengthy and expensive, so seek professional advice from a solicitor first.

Private treatment
Complaints about services not provided under the NHS can be made to the British College of Ophthalmic Opticians or the Association of Optical Practitioners if one of their own members is involved.

Spectacle frames and lenses sold privately are considered ordinary consumer goods, so all the customer's rights under the Sale of Goods Act 1979 apply (see page 13). You could also ask the Society of Opticians to investigate complaints involving frames and lenses when one of their members (probably one of the large chains) is concerned. The Guild of British Dispensing Opticians might be able to help when a smaller firm has supplied unsatisfactory private glasses.

COMPLAINTS ABOUT PHARMACISTS

In general, if you have a complaint against a pharmacist and feel you need help and advice, ask your district Community Health Council[12] – their services are free.

Pharmacists, like doctors and dentists, are answerable to two different bodies:

■ their professional body, **the Pharmaceutical Society of Great Britain**.[13] Anyone wishing to practise as a pharmacist must be on the register of Pharmaceutical Chemists maintained by the Society, and must abide by its rules and standards

■ the local **Family Practitioner Committee**,[14] the administrative machine of the NHS for pharmacists, dentists, opticians and doctors (GPs). It is with the FPC that the pharmacist has his contract of service. Look in the phone book for the local address.

Complaints to the Pharmaceutical Society

The Society not only deals with complaints about professional misconduct and ethics but is also empowered to enforce certain sections of the Medicines Act 1968.[15] For example the Society has powers under the Act to bring a prosecution against a pharmacist where the medicine supplied 'was not of the nature and quality demanded'. A written complaint of this or indeed of any other nature can be made to the Society. You should include:

■ the name and address of the pharmacist who supplied the medicine, and of the doctor who prescribed it
■ details of your complaint. **Do not** send the drugs through the post; retain them for now

An inspector from the society will visit you and take further particulars. He will also take statements from all the other relevant people – the pharmacist, perhaps a member of his staff, and the doctor who wrote the prescription. The statements will be submitted along with a report to the Chief Inspector who can, depending on the facts:

■ issue a warning letter to the pharmacist
■ submit the details to the Law Committee of the Society's elected council which decides whether the Society will prosecute
■ submit the matter to the Ethics Committee where the problem is primarily a professional matter, for example one of attitude and ability. The Ethics Committee will decide whether the issue should be referred to the Society's disciplinary council, the Statutory Committee. The Statutory Committee may conduct a formal hearing and, if appropriate, remove a person's name from the register of pharmaceutical chemists

Complaints to the local Family Practitioner Committee[14]

If your complaint is about the supply of medicines under the National Health Service, or one where you believe a pharmacist might be in breach of some aspect of his contract of service, such as by closing his shop early, you can complain to the local Family Practitioner Committee.

An investigation will be made and where appropriate the pharmacist will be brought to a hearing. If the pharmacist is found in breach of his NHS contract, the Family Practitioner Committee has powers to take disciplinary action against him.

Compensation

Neither the Pharmaceutical Society of Great Britain nor your local Family Practitioner Committee has any power to award compensation to a complainant, even when it has been established that the complaint is justified. If compensation is what you want you must think about taking legal action against the pharmacist. Seek proper legal advice first.

COMPLAINTS ABOUT THE PROFESSIONS

COMPLAINTS ABOUT ACCOUNTANTS

If you have a complaint against an accountant, complain to his professional body – a simple and accurate procedure in theory, but in practice a little more complex.

There are several professional accountancy bodies in the country. Which one you complain to will depend on the association to which the particular accountant belongs. It will be one of these:

- the Institute of Chartered Accountants in England and Wales
- the Institute of Chartered Accountants of Scotland
- the Ulster branch of the Institute of Chartered Accountants of Ireland
- the Association of Certified Accountants
- the Institute of Cost and Management Accountants
- the Chartered Institute of Public Finance and Accountancy
- the Institute of Chartered Secretaries and Administrators

These are the steps to take if you want to register an effective complaint about an accountant:

- First of all raise the matter yourself with the accountant concerned. Tell him you are dissatisfied with his work for a particular reason and see what his response is. Very often a complaint can be resolved immediately.
- If this does not achieve what you want, as a second step you could write a formal letter of complaint to the senior partner who will certainly look into the matter.
- If you still have no luck, you should refer the matter to the accountant's professional body. Which association your accountant belongs to ought to be clear from his letterhead, but you could otherwise ring his office and ask. Make your complaint formally in writing, giving as many relevant details as possible and sending copies of the correspondence.

Each association has its own disciplinary codes to which its members should adhere, and its own procedures for dealing with complaints. The procedures are geared towards obtaining as much evidence as possible about the issues in question and seeing both sides of the case. Only after these preliminary investigations will it be decided whether the complaint is to be investigated further and dealt with by the association's various disciplinary committees; they will then decide what (if any) action should be taken against the accountant involved.

If the matter gives rise to questions of public concern, it will be investigated by the relatively new 'Joint Disciplinary Scheme' operated by the three main accountancy bodies.

While there is a highly organised system for investigating complaints, and a willingness to discipline those accountants in breach of their association's established codes of professional conduct, none can award compensation to a complainant. So if you feel that your accountant has been negligent in some way, and you want to seek compensation, you must think about legal action in Court. Get professional legal advice first.

COMPLAINTS ABOUT INSURANCE BROKERS

In the simplest terms an insurance broker is a person who advises on and arranges insurance for his clients. Brokers usually earn their living out of commission paid to them by insurance companies when business is introduced to them. If you have a complaint against an insurance broker there are two different channels for pursuing it:

■ the British Insurance Brokers' Association (BIBA)
■ the Insurance Brokers' Registration Council

If your complaint is over some aspect of your policy, see page 109.

The British Insurance Brokers' Association
First of all take the matter up with the insurance broker. If this proves unsuccessful write to the Consumer Relations Officer at the British Insurance Brokers' Association (BIBA). This is the national trade association which will investigate complaints against members, offer a conciliation service, and where necessary take disciplinary action. In your letter give as much detail about your complaint as possible and enclose copies of any relevant correspondence. The Consumer Relations Officer will then ask the insurance broker for his side of the story. The problem often turns out to be one of poor communication rather than of misconduct or negligence on the part of the broker. However, when there is evidence of misconduct or repeated negligence, this information is passed to the Membership and Investigations Committee which may in turn pass the matter to a Disciplinary Committee which has powers to expel a member from BIBA.

The Insurance Brokers' Registration Council
Since 1981 anyone wishing to use the description 'insurance broker' must be registered with the Insurance Brokers' Registration Council. Once registered, insurance brokers must comply with the code of conduct. The Council has a duty to investigate complaints from the public and the power to remove an insurance broker from the Register which it maintains. In addition to this the Council also has a compensatory function.

When do you complain to the Council?
If the insurance broker is a member of BIBA, and if you have been unable to resolve matters with the individual broker concerned, refer your complaint

to BIBA. There are three circumstances, however, when it is advisable to refer your complaint straight to the Insurance Brokers' Registration Council:

- when the insurance broker involved is not a member of BIBA
- when it becomes clear that the matter is not one that can be swiftly resolved by BIBA, or if you are unhappy with the way they are handling it
- when it becomes evident that BIBA will be passing details of your complaint to its Membership and Investigations Committee

Put your complaint to the Registrar of the Insurance Brokers' Registration Council in writing, giving as much detail as possible and enclosing any relevant correspondence.

COMPLAINTS ABOUT STOCKBROKERS

As well as buying and selling shares on behalf of their clients, stockbrokers advise individuals, companies and institutions wanting to invest money on a whole range of financial topics.

If you have a complaint to make about a stockbroker,[16] take the matter up with the individual broker. To do so is simply a matter of courtesy – after all it is reasonable that you should give the person you are complaining about a chance to sort things out before you take any more drastic action. In any case, the Stock Exchange, of which all stockbrokers are members, will not look into a complaint until they are satisfied that you have attempted to resolve the matter with the individual broker.

Where this proves unsatisfactory, write a letter (keeping a copy) to the Complaints Section at the Stock Exchange. Give full details of your complaint and make sure that you mention the name of the broker you have been dealing with, and the name of his firm.

The Stock Exchange will investigate the matter, and will of course give the person you are complaining about an opportunity to offer his comments on your allegations. Where they feel a complaint is justified they will bring to bear what influence they have on the broker in order to get him to resolve the issue satisfactorily.

They also have a set of disciplinary rules to which all their members must adhere. Where the complaint suggests that a breach of these rules has taken place, an investigating panel will be set up to discover whether this is the case. Where definite breaches of the rules have taken place, the Stock Exchange has a variety of disciplinary powers ranging from a private reprimand to expulsion. Although this procedure would not achieve anything tangible for you the complainant, it might act as useful evidence if you decided to take legal action against a stockbroker.

However, in order to protect investors, the Stock Exchange has set up a compensation fund to recompense clients who lose money as a result of a stockbroker's actions. A booklet setting out the circumstances in which this compensation is payable is available free from the Stock Exchange.

COMPLAINTS ABOUT LICENSED DEALERS

A licensed dealer is a person who has a special licence granted by the Department of Trade to act for people buying and selling shares. If you have a complaint about a licensed dealer direct it to the Department of Trade and not to the Stock Exchange.

COMPLAINTS ABOUT ARCHITECTS

Architects are subject to three controlling influences in the way they behave, each one providing a channel through which a member of the public can register an effective complaint:

- **The Architects' Registration Council of the United Kingdom** (ARCUK) This is a statutory body with whom all practising architects must be registered. It can investigate complaints made against any of its 28,000 registered architects where there is some indication of 'disgraceful conduct'.
- **The Royal Institute of British Architects** (RIBA)[17] This is the architects' professional body. It lays down a code of professional conduct to which all its 27,000 members must adhere, and any complaint involving a possible breach of its standards will be fully investigated
- **The law** When you employ an architect to undertake a specific job, you enter into a legally binding contract with him, so to prevent any disputes make sure that you have agreed on all the important details of the contract before the work is started. It is implicit in the contract that the price charged, the standard of work performed and the time taken must all be reasonable. Complaints about contracts of services are dealt with in detail on page 33. If you have a complaint about what amounts to a contractual matter you must look to the law and the Courts for your remedy. RIBA and ARCUK cannot help you as their authority extends only to dealing with complaints involving ethical matters.

How to complain

If you have a complaint about professional misconduct on the part of an architect, give him a reasonable opportunity to sort things out first. Explain your concern to him in writing and ask him to remedy whatever you feel is wrong. It is highly likely that he will either put things right immediately, or give you an acceptable explanation about his actions.

If this does not resolve things to your satisfaction, and if the architect is a member of RIBA (it will usually say so on his notepaper), write to RIBA's regional

65

office for your area. If the problem seems basically to be a breakdown in communications between you and the architect, RIBA will attempt to resolve the situation at regional level, but a complaint of a more serious ethical nature will be passed to the head office.

Alternatively, you can send your complaint direct to RIBA's head office yourself, and allow them to determine who should deal with it. They will conduct a comprehensive investigation into your complaint, which is likely to take between three and six months. All parties are given the opportunity to present their side of the case. Ultimately, if the alleged complaint is proved against the architect, he will be disciplined. He may receive a warning, a suspension, or in extreme cases he may be expelled from RIBA.

Note that RIBA has no power to award a successful complainant any compensation. If this is what you are after, seek legal advice about taking your case to Court.

If RIBA believes that the architect's behaviour constitutes 'disgraceful conduct', it may refer the matter to ARCUK, who may itself conduct an investigation with a view to possible disciplinary action in the form of striking him off the register.

If an architect is not a member of RIBA, complain to ARCUK yourself, after attempting to resolve the matter informally with the architect involved. You would have to established that the architect was guilty of 'disgraceful conduct' in order for ARCUK to discipline the person concerned. RIBA maintains a list of architects willing to help over negligence cases.

As a final tip, if you are in doubt about how or where to complain about an architect, write to RIBA: they will at least point you in the right direction.

COMPLAINTS ABOUT CHARTERED SURVEYORS

All those who practise as chartered surveyors must be members of the Royal Institution of Chartered Surveyors. Being so registered means that an individual chartered surveyor is subject to all the rules of professional conduct and to the disciplinary powers and procedures of the Royal Institution, their professional body.

If you have a complaint, write to the Professional Practices Department, sending any documentary evidence necessary. You should also include your permission to forward a copy of the letter and of the enclosures to the subject of the complaint. If the complaint is found to be justified, the Institution may expel, suspend or reprimand the chartered surveyor concerned.

The Institution has no power to assess or award compensation for professional negligence. If this is what you want seek the advice of a solicitor with a view to taking legal action.

Complaints about surveys

If you feel that a survey has not been properly carried out and that as a result you have suffered loss you may be able to sue the surveyor for breach of contract: under the Supply of Goods and Services Act 1982[18] a service must be performed to a reasonable standard.

Where a building society or bank employs a surveyor to inspect a property you are considering buying, although you don't have a contract with the surveyor, it may still be possible to take action against him for negligence. You should seek the professional advice of a solicitor.

COMPLAINTS ABOUT ESTATE AGENTS

All chartered surveyors are entitled to call themselves estate agents and to act as such. The opposite is not true: an estate agent cannot call himself a chartered surveyor, or act as one, if he is not a member of the Royal Institution of Chartered Surveyors. You might want to check this before employing an estate agent.

Some estate agents are members of the National Association of Estate Agents, who will handle enquiries and complaints about its members. But if you feel you have suffered some loss because of the way an estate agent has handled your affairs, you could raise your complaint with the local Trading Standards Department,[19] or else see a solicitor with a view to taking legal action.

Notes: Scotland and Northern Ireland

1 Scotland and Northern Ireland each has its own Law Society (see address list).

2 If your complaint to the Scottish Law Society cannot be resolved through correspondence, the case will be referred to the Complaints Committee. This Committee may recommend the Society to refer the complaint to the Discipline Tribunal, an independent body with the power to fine or suspend a solicitor, or, in extreme cases, to have him struck off the roll of solicitors. You may also complain directly to the Discipline Tribunal, but if you are unsuccessful you may have to pay expenses.

3 Neither the Law Society of Scotland nor the Law Society of Northern Ireland deals with allegations of negligence.

   The Law Society of Scotland has a similar panel of solicitors to the 'negligence panel' known as 'troubleshooters'. It also has a guarantee fund to compensate those who have lost money through a solicitor's dishonesty.

   If you have difficulty in finding a solicitor in Northern Ireland who is willing to take a 'negligence' case against another solicitor, the Law Society of Northern Ireland will help in finding a senior solicitor willing to advise and assist you.

4 The Law Society of Scotland does not arbitrate on fees. They issue a table of fees but this is only a general guide. If you are not satisfied with your solicitor's explanation of his charges, you may have the bill taxed by the Auditor of Court. You will usually have to pay for the service.

   Complaints about a solicitor's fees in Northern Ireland may be directed to that country's Law Society. Alternatively, advice on the procedure for taxation of costs may be obtained from the Master (Taxing) – see address list – or from any local County Court office.

5 The Lay Observer in Edinburgh deals with complaints about the Law Society in Scotland. He has no authority when it comes to considering complaints about Scottish advocates. The same applies to the Lay Observer of the Law Society of Northern Ireland.

6 In Scotland, advocates are the equivalent of barristers. There is no system of Inns of Court or Chambers. If you have a complaint about the conduct of an advocate, you should made it to the Dean of Faculty (the leader of the Scottish bar). Legal action against an advocate is likely to prove as fruitless as action against a barrister in England.

   The Chambers system does not operate in Northern Ireland either. You should direct any complaints about Northern Irish barristers to the Bar Council at the Royal Courts of Justice in Belfast.

7 Family Practitioner Committees do not exist in Scotland or Northern Ireland. Complaints about poor service from your GP in Scotland should go to the administrator of the Primary Care Division of the Area Health Board. In Northern Ireland such complaints are dealt with by the Central Services Agency.

8 In Scotland you need to make any complaint about your GP to the Area Health Board within six weeks.

9 The Scottish counterpart of the Community Health Council is the Local Health Council; in Northern Ireland you can get advice from the Central Services Agency.

10 The Area Health Board is the Scottish equivalent of the English Family Practitioner Committee. Complaints about dentists in Northern Ireland are dealt with by the Central Services Agency.

11 In Scotland, complaints about opticians that in England would go to the Family Practitioner Committee should be addressed to the administrator of the Primary Care Division of the Area Health Board.

   If you have a complaint to do with an optician or his services in Northern Ireland, contact the Central Services Agency for an NHS matter, or the General Optical Council for a service provided privately.

12 The Scottish counterpart of the Community Health Council is the Local Health Council; in Northern Ireland you get advice about pharmacists from the Central Services Agency.

13 Anyone wishing to practise as a pharmacist in Northern Ireland must be on the register maintained by the Pharmaceutical Society of Northern Ireland.

14 The Area Health Board is the Scottish equivalent of the Family Practitioner Committee. Complaints about pharmacists in Northern Ireland are dealt with by the Central Services Agency.

15 The power to enforce the Medicines Act lies in Northern Ireland with the Department of Health and Social Services, not with the Pharmaceutical Society.

16 Complaints concerning stockbrokers in Northern Ireland may be directed either to the Stock Exchange in London or to the General Manager at the Stock Exchange in Belfast.

17 The Royal Incorporation of Architects in Scotland (RIAS) is a separate body but closely associated with RIBA. A complaint made to RIAS about an architect who is not a member of that body would be passed on to RIBA for attention.

18 The Supply of Goods and Services Act 1982 does not apply in Scotland but you may be able to sue a surveyor there for breach of contract under common law.

19 In Northern Ireland the equivalent of the Trading Standards Department is the Trading Standards Branch of the Department of Economic Development for Northern Ireland.

Complaints about public corporations

COMPLAINTS ABOUT ELECTRICITY

The most common complaint electricity consumers have is over bills – in most cases this means that they do not accept the meter reading. Threats of disconnection may follow and in turn lead to additional disputes. Other common complaints arise from clerical errors or failure to reply to letters, or involve service and supply (rudeness in the showrooms, faulty appliances bought from one of the Boards).

Before enlisting any help you should approach your particular district of the Electricity Board[1] and give them a chance to sort things out. Ring the number given on your bill or call at the local showroom. Make sure you keep a record of the date, what happens, and to whom you speak.

The Area Electricity Consultative Councils

If you are not satisfied with the response you get from the Board, ask your Area Electricity Consultative Council to take up the matter on your behalf. There are twelve Consultative Councils within the areas of the twelve Electricity Boards (plus two in Scotland). They deal with complaints brought to them by consumers who are not satisfied with the way their problems have been handled by their Board. Addresses are given on the backs of bills and are displayed in Electricity Board shops (see also the address section).

The Electricity Council

If you are still dissatisfied when this particular route has been explored, and if the Area Consultative Council echoes your dissatisfaction, it may refer the complaint to the Electricity Council.[2] If the Consultative Council does not wish to do this, you may refer the matter yourself. The Electricity Council is the body which formulates the overall policy for the electricity supply industry in England and Wales and is the principal channel for consultation between the electricity supply industry and government. The Council will hold a hearing on your complaint and will make a decision. If you or the Consultative Council find the decision unsatisfactory, either of you can refer the matter to the Secretary of State who has powers to give a direction to the Board.

Particular disputes

If you think that **your electricity bill is too much,** you have the right to have the meter checked. You should ask your Electricity Board to send one of their officials to do this. A meter is deemed to be accurate if it registers within a tolerance of $+2\frac{1}{2}\%$ and $-3\frac{1}{2}\%$. If you are still dissatisfied after this check has been carried out, you are entitled to approach the Department of Energy. They will send one of their inspectors and his decision is final and legally binding. There is no fee for this service. You would be well advised to seek the guidance of your Area Electricity Consultative Council over this.

Another area of complaint – one in which the law can help – involves **faulty goods bought from an Electricity Board.** Your legal rights here are contained in the Sale of Goods Act 1979 – see the section on Complaints over Goods on page 11.

In certain circumstances you may have a legal remedy against an Electricity Board if it is in breach of its legal obligations. For example, **the Boards must supply electricity to anyone who asks for it** provided they are within a certain statutory distance of the point of supply. The Boards are also empowered to disconnect you for failure to pay, but in doing so they must abide by strict and highly technical regulations and a Code of Practice agreed upon between the Electricity Consumers' Council (see below) and the Department of Energy (the Code covers all the fuel industries). Seek expert advice for a possible legal remedy. The Area Consultative Council or the Citizens Advice Bureau will also be able to help.

The Electricity Consumers' Council[3]

This was set up in 1977 to represent at national level the interests of electricity consumers in England and Wales. It does not handle individual complaints but deals with issues of national importance such as energy conservation and price changes, through which all consumers are affected.

COMPLAINTS ABOUT GAS

As with electricity the most common complaint that gas consumers have is over bills – in other words they are not confident that their meter is accurate. Other complaints concern the quality or lack of service (an engineer failing to turn up on time, or forgetting to bring the right tools with him, or not doing the job properly), and the quality of goods bought from a British Gas showroom.

If you have cause for complaint start by asking your district Gas Board to sort it out by ringing the number on your bill or by calling at the local showroom. Keep a record of dates and conversations.

British Gas Regional Boards[4]

If you need to pursue your case further write to the Regional Chairman of the Board – his address is usually on the backs of bills. British Gas is divided into twelve Regional Boards, each one having a Chairman who is ultimately responsible for the gas services provided by his Region. If your complaint is justified it will probably be dealt with very quickly. But if the response proves unsatisfactory and it appears that you are going to have a battle on your hands, bring in your Regional Gas Consumers' Council.

National Gas Consumers' Council[4]

The Council was set up to represent at national level the interests of the consumer over disputes and complaints about gas services. Each locality has a Regional Gas Consumers' Council – addresses can be found in the address section and are also usually shown on gas bills.

Make your complaint in writing, preferably on a typewriter.

Particular disputes

If you believe that your meter is not registering correctly and thus **your bills are too high**, ask your Gas Region to arrange for an independent check to be carried out by the Department of Energy. They will send one of their inspectors and his decision is final and legally binding.

The Gas Boards are obliged to supply you with gas, providing you don't owe them money. If they fail to honour this obligation by cutting you off when you have paid your bill or when they have not gone through the correct procedures over a disconnection even though for legitimate reasons, you should remind them that they are in breach of their statutory obligation and that they could be prosecuted and fined.

Like any other organisation providing a service for money, the gas boards are subject to the law of contract: they must honour their promises and do what they agreed to do. They must, for example, under your agreement with them, turn up on time. If you told them that failure to arrive at a particular time or on a particular day would cause you to incur expense, you can claim this. They must perform the job to a reasonable standard and failure to do so will render them liable to breach of contract. Action will be taken against them in the same way that action would be taken against anyone **failing to provide the agreed services** (see page 33).

If goods and appliances bought from British Gas prove unsatisfactory in some way, your rights are exactly the same as with goods bought from anyone else in business. Most of these rights are contained in the Sale of Goods Act 1979, and are dealt with in the section on Complaints over Goods.

COMPLAINTS ABOUT COAL

The organisation which represents consumer interests in the solid fuel industry is the domestic Coal Consumers' Council. The Council is independent from the National Coal Board and its members are appointed by the Secretary of State. It has close links with the Approved Coal Merchants Scheme (see below) and has encouraged the introduction of Codes of Practice covering the industry.

The Council advises that complaints or queries go first to your coal merchant. If he is in the Approved Coal Merchants Scheme he is obliged to help you as much as he can.

If you are not satisfied get in touch with the Solid Fuel Advisory Service[5] or the Regional Secretary of the Approved Coal Merchants Scheme (see the address section).

Finally the Council itself will help. It does not advertise itself specifically as a complaints handling organisation but it can help over 'adequacy of supplies;

standards of service; prices and quality of solid fuel; all aspects of the present and future use of solid fuel to heat the home and general matters of consumer protection affecting solid fuel users'.

COMPLAINTS ABOUT WATER

No consumer council exists for dealing with complaints about the water industry. If you can't sort out your problem with your local water authority, contact the local government Ombudsman (see page 91).[6]

COMPLAINTS ABOUT THE POST OFFICE AND BRITISH TELECOM

The Post Office

The most common complaints about the Post Office are delays in delivery and loss or damage to the contents of the mail. The Post Office is not legally liable for anything that happens to the mail unless you have sent your letter by registered mail, or your parcel under a special insurance scheme, where compensation will be paid if the parcel is lost or damaged. The amount of compensation will depend on how much you agreed to pay for the service.

In addition to the terms of registered delivery, the Post Office has to adhere to a Postal Code of Practice which contains provisions for compensation payable in some specified circumstances. This is thought to have helped reduce the number of such complaints. Whether you want to make a claim or raise a matter of lost or damaged mail, a special form available at any Post Office should be completed. Even though the Post Office isn't liable in law for mail any complaint made in the correct way to the local Head Postmaster will be investigated.

What else can you do?

Generally if you want to make a complaint about any aspect of the Post Office's services you should write first to the Head Postmaster for your area. If that doesn't produce satisfactory results write to the Regional Director, then the Managing Director (postal) at the London headquarters, and finally the Chairman of the Post Office. The addresses of your Head Postmaster and Regional Director can be obtained from your local Post Office.

Note too that most regions have their own full-time public relations officer who tries to keep customers happy – again, his address will be found at the Post Office.

Further sources of help may be your local Post Office Advisory Committee and the Post Office Users' National Council[7] (see page 75).

Complaints about British Telecom

British Telecom has a statutory monopoly to administer the telecommunications network in Britain (apart from in Hull where there is an independent telephone service). If you have a complaint try to deal with the person most likely to be in a position to do something about it.

- If your telephone has a **crackle** or is generally out of order, and calls to 151 and the Exchange Engineer turn out to be fruitless, a letter to the Area Engineer should help.
- Ask the operator to deduct any **crossed line calls** from your meter charges.
- If you want to complain about **your bill** (which is, incidentally, the most common ground for complaint over telephones) write to the Area Accountant.
- If there are problems over an **installation**, or alterations or additions to an existing connection, the Sales and Installations Manager is your man.
- If you feel the **general standard of service is poor**, or if the operator has sworn at you, complain to the Service Manager.
- If none of these people can sort you out, or if you are not happy with the way your complaint is being dealt with, write to the General Manager of your region. Outline why you are not satisfied, and tell him what you would like him to do.

The address for all these people is care of the General Manager – see the information section at the front of the telephone directory.

Above the General Manager is the Regional Director and above him the Managing Director (Telecommunications) at the London head office.

Who can help?

Whether your complaint concerns the Post Office or British Telecom, there are two other organisations who may be able to help.

There are nearly 200 Post Office Advisory Committees (POACs) spread somewhat haphazardly throughout the UK. They are increasingly called POTACs to take British Telecom into account. Their function is to liaise with local Post Office and Telecom management and the general public and to assist the Post Office Users' National Council (see below) in ascertaining the opinion of users. Whatever the nature of your problem or complaint with or against the Post Office or British Telecom, enlist the support and advice of the POTAC for your locality – ask at your Post Office for their address.

The Post Office Users' National Council (POUNC)[8] was set up to receive complaints from Post Office and British Telecom users and see that representations are properly made, received and dealt with through the appropriate channels. The Council is mainly concerned with general issues such as proposed price increases, but will help with individual cases on condition that you have first tried to help yourself by at least contacting the local postmaster or Telecom manager. It will need from you a full statement, with which you should send copies of any relevant correspondence.

If you're in doubt whether or not to refer the matter to POUNC bear in mind a short paragraph from one of their recent annual reports:

The complaints POUNC receives represent a small proportion of those submitted by customers to the Post Office and British Telecom. Nevertheless they give us a valuable insight into the customer viewpoint on a wide range of issues. We use them to pursue customers' interests on an individual basis. They also provide the key for comment on those performance and price issues of a broad policy nature on specific services which we take up with Posts and Telecom.

If POUNC can't help, get hold of a copy of the Code of Practice (available at Post and Telecom Offices) which details the complaints procedure and will inform you how to get the case dealt with by independent arbitration.

Notes: Scotland and Northern Ireland

1 In Northern Ireland start trying to resolve any dispute by going to the local office of the Northern Ireland Electricity Service (see also page 26).

2 There is no organisation corresponding to the Electricity Council in Scotland.

3 There is no organisation corresponding to the Electricity Consumers' Council in Scotland. In Northern Ireland the N.I. Electricity Consumers' Council deals with individual complaints, unlike the English counterpart.

4 British Gas does not operate in Northern Ireland, and there is no Gas Consumers' Council either. Complaints should be made to the Northern Ireland Gas Employers' Board or to the local Town Gas office. More general complaints could be made to the Northern Ireland Consumers' Council.

5 Complaints should be directed either to the Northern Ireland Coal Advisory Service or to the Trading Standards Branch of the Department of Economic Development for Northern Ireland.

6 In Scotland, the Regional and Islands Councils are the Water Authorities; complaints should be directed to the relevant Council.
    In Northern Ireland, complaints should go to the Department of the Environment for Northern Ireland.

7 Scotland and Northern Ireland each has its own Post Office Users' Council.

8 The Customer Relations Department of British Telecom in Belfast deals with Northern Irish complaints.

Complaints about local authorities

A great many of the services we all take for granted are provided by the local authority: from public transport to evening classes and care facilities for the elderly and the disabled, the local authority takes on many and varied responsibilities. It is of course inevitable that from time to time complaints will arise. Making an effective complaint against a local authority can be a formidable task, so the purpose of this section of the book is to present some relevant general information on the subject and then to examine complaints procedures concerning specific services such as rating, housing and planning.

A GENERAL GUIDE TO LOCAL GOVERNMENT ORGANISATION

Some local authority services are provided by County Councils[1] or, in heavily populated areas, Metropolitan County Councils, while other services are provided by District or Metropolitan District Councils. Clearly the first step in registering an effective complaint is to discover whether it is the County or the District Council which is responsible for the particular service. A call to the Citizens Advice Bureau should help with this.

For the sake of simplicity there are six identifiable levels of complaint. Which level you begin with largely depends on the seriousness of the matter and what you have to gain by complaining.

The man on the job

The most basic level of complaint is to the person performing the service. Remember that such a person's power will probably be limited, so there is little point in giving full vent to your frustration to someone not really in a position to do anything about it. For example, there is no point in complaining to the road-digger about the position of a particular hole when he has been asked to dig in that spot. But if while he is digging the hole he causes a nuisance by swearing or playing a radio at full blast for several hours, he would obviously be the most appropriate person to complain to.

The man on the job's boss

Where it is pointless complaining to the man on the job, or when such a course of action has been fruitless, you should put your complaint in writing to the person's boss – the Chief Officer for that department, for example the Director of Education, the Chief Planning Officer etc. Although he will be anxious to protect his staff from criticism and unjustified or trivial complaints, it is also his duty to look into complaints by the general public, and if one is justified he must take appropriate action.

The Chief Executive

This person goes by a variety of titles in different parts of the country such as Chief Executive Officer, Town Clerk, City Manager, and is basically responsible for the smooth running of all the various administrative and legal functions of a local authority. He will also be interested to hear of grievances against any of the departments that go to make up a local authority. Who and where he is can be found out by contacting the Citizens Advice Bureau.

District Auditor

This person fulfils an important but little-known role. As previous Acts before it, the Local Government Act 1972[2] imposes an obligation on all local authorities to have their accounts scrutinised by an approved District Auditor. In a way the District Auditor acts as something of a watchdog for the ratepayer. Apart from satisfying himself that correct and proper accounting practices have been adopted, he is under a duty to make sure that individual items of the account are not contrary to the law. Previous cases have shown for example that excessive and unjustifiable expenditure is contrary to the law.

So anyone who feels that the way a local authority is utilising ratepayers' money is excessive or unjustified may complain in writing to the District Auditor. Where he feels that any item of the account is contrary to the law, he will make a special application to the High Court to this effect. The Court may order the person responsible for ordering the unlawful expenditure to repay all or part of it.

The Councillor

Local authorities' policies are formulated by councillors elected by the community. The local authority officer responsible for the various departments, while acting in an advisory capacity to the councillors on a particular matter, is clearly under an obligation to carry out the council's decisions which have been properly and democratically made. Where you have a complaint about an issue of general policy or the way policy has been interpreted, contact the councillor, preferably the one elected to serve the area you live in. In this way the councillors are able to raise complaints in the most appropriate quarter. If you aren't sure whom to contact, get the name of the right person from the Town Hall or equivalent local authority headquarters. The Citizens Advice Bureau can also help with names and addresses.

The Local Government Ombudsman[3]

The Commission for Local Administration was created by the Local Government Act 1974. Local commissioners, or Ombudsmen as they are usually called, investigate complaints of maladministration by local authorities. The Commission was set up specifically to provide an easily accessible complaints procedure, so it is worth knowing about it (see page 91).

COMPLAINTS ABOUT RATES

Local government derives a very large proportion of its funds from the rates. If you are an occupier of property you are liable to pay rates. The amount you pay is based on the kind of property you are occupying and its area.

Excessive rates

If you think you are paying too much there are two initial courses of action open to you:

- apply for a rate reduction
- apply for a rate rebate

Applying for a rate reduction

You may think that the amount you have to pay is excessive either because your neighbour is paying less for living in a similar house with the same facilities; alternatively, changes in the neighbourhood may have affected the desirability of the area, such as a new airport with its incoming flightpath directly over your house, a bus route now passing your house, or a new bridge bringing a dramatic increase of traffic to your area. Where something like this has occurred you should apply for a rate reduction. The procedure is as follows:

- Contact your local valuation office[4] which is usually based at the same premises as your local tax office. You can check the address in the phone book under Inland Revenue. Tell them that you wish to apply for a rate reduction and that you require the appropriate form. Technically, you are going to 'make a proposal to alter the valuation list'.

- Complete the 'proposal' form giving details of why you think your rates should be reduced.
- A valuation officer will look at your application. If he agrees to a reduction, and you agree to the amount, that is the end of the matter. If he objects, or if you can't agree on the amount of the reduction, your case can go to the local valuation court, whose ultimate decision is binding. If your case does get to this stage you would be well advised to seek professional legal advice.

Applying for a rate rebate

You may think that the amount of your rates is fair and reasonable taking into account the type of house and all the other relevant factors, but that it is excessive when viewed against your income. In this case you should apply for a rate rebate. The form for this is available from the rating authority and the Citizens Advice Bureau.

When you have completed and returned the form, the authority applies a means-tested formula weighing your income against your expenditure. Note that if you are granted a rate rebate, although in practice you will be paying less, the rateable value of the property will not have altered. Income limits are reviewed quite often so that new groups of people, particularly senior citizens, may qualify for a rebate. Rebates are not retrospective, so it's important to apply for one as soon as you qualify. If your income then increases you must notify the authority who will recalculate the amount payable.

COMPLAINTS ABOUT COUNCIL HOUSING

If you have any complaint about council housing matters,[5] you should complain to the District Council as it is responsible for housing facilities and services. The law relating to this topic and the obligations that a local authority owes to the general public are vast and complicated, so a knowledge of the particular legal rules involved in any given situation may prove to be the key to successful resolution of a complaint. This section of the book therefore sets out merely to list the main bodies or places where you can seek help and advice, and to give some broad guidelines and tips on how to go about handling some of the most common and serious complaints.

Where to get help

- **The Citizens Advice Bureau** There is likely to be one fairly close to where you live. It can give advice on general housing matters, supply you with free leaflets on the topic, or at least point you towards more detailed and positive assistance.

- **Housing Aid and Advice Centres** These are set up in many towns and cities by the local authorities themselves, specifically to advise and answer general queries about housing matters. Many centres now publish their own action kits.
- **The National Tenants' Organisation** This organisation can give you general advice and assist you to form your own tenants' association. A group of people with similar complaints has more bargaining power than an individual.
- **Shelter** This is a voluntary pressure group who can advise you on virtually all housing matters and will sometimes take up a complaint on your behalf. Its headquarters are in London and there are several regional offices. If you have what you consider to be a genuinely serious problem or complaint against a local housing department, this is probably the best organisation to contact.

Complaints and how to deal with them

The way in which you might handle specific problems will largely depend on the type of complaint you have and the degree to which you are being deprived of your legal rights. It would be impossible to go into detail about all the sorts of complaints reported to the local government Ombudsman, so the remainder of this section is devoted to just two of the most common and serious complaints:

- failure by a council to house
- failure by a council to maintain property according to legal requirements

Failure to house

The Housing (Homeless Persons) Act 1977[6] provides that local authorities are under a legal duty to help people who are homeless or who fear that they may shortly become homeless. For the purposes of this Act a person is regarded as being homeless if:

- they are without a place to stay the night
- they have been turned out of where they were staying
- they have had to leave their home for fear of violence from someone living there

The extent of help that a local authority will give varies enormously according to the circumstances. For example, it must find accommodation, even if only temporary, for people who have a 'priority' need, such as those with young children, pregnant women, old people, the disabled, and anyone made homeless by some emergency. On the other hand, providing help for people outside these priority categories may simply amount to giving general advice and may fall short of actually providing accommodation.

When approached for help the council must either agree to help and find you accommodation or refuse to help but give you the reasons. If you feel that you are not being given the help you are legally entitled to, there is no formal appeals procedure for immediate review of your case. All you can do is to write to the local authority's Director of Housing stating that you are dissatisfied with the way the department has dealt with you and asking him to review your case. Failing any success, you should contact your local councillor and ask him to take up the matter on your behalf. As a final resort you could complain to the Local Government Ombudsman (see page 91).

Failure to maintain the property

If you are a council tenant, your landlord is the local authority. The law imposes upon it certain basic obligations such as the responsibility for some of the maintenance and repair work to the property. The Housing Act 1961[7] states that the local authority is responsible for:

- repairs to the overall structure of the building, such as floors, roof, walls and windows
- maintenance of gutters and drainage
- maintenance of general service facilities, such as electrical and gas piping and wiring
- maintenance of the plumbing facilities

These are the minimum standards; some local authorities take on additional obligations which will be set out in the tenancy agreement. Ask the Housing Department for a copy of it so that you can check.

How to get the authority to do repairs

Inform them in writing that the work needs doing and give them reasonable time and opportunity to do it. Some authorities have special forms for you to complete so check first whether this is necessary. Keep copies of your initial request.

If the work is not done within a reasonable time you could consider one of three further courses of action:

- Obtain estimates from a number of local tradesmen and select the cheapest. Write to the Housing Department again, this time enclosing a copy of the estimate, informing them that if they do not have the work done within seven days you will have it done yourself and that you will deduct the costs from the rent. If you do have to take this course of action, revert to paying the full rent as soon as you have deducted your repair bill.
- Get in touch with the local authority's Environmental Health Department and ask one of their inspectors to visit. Inform him of the work that needs to be done and of the council's failure to do it. The Inspector himself has no absolute powers to make the council do the work (except when you are a GLC tenant) but he can generally apply some pressure from within.
- As the council is in breach of its legal obligations by failing to do repair work for which it is responsible, you can take legal action to compel it to do the work and possibly to claim damages. If the repair work is of a fairly major nature this is probably the best channel to pursue.

In any event **do not** simply refuse to pay the rent. All this achieves is to put you in breach of your legal obligations too, which can only lead to more trouble.

Taking legal action[8]

Legal action could be taken under the Public Health Act 1936, the Housing Act 1957, or the Housing Acts of 1961 and 1980. Which one you would base your action on will depend on the type of repairs involved and the remedy you are seeking. Do not dabble in this without getting expert legal advice first.

COMPLAINTS ABOUT PLANNING

In many cases the law provides specific channels for pursuing complaints about planning matters. Much of this section is devoted to explaining these procedures and the circumstances in which they are applicable.

Where planning permission is refused

If you want to alter an existing building substantially, build a new one, or indeed just make a 'material change of use' of land or a building, you need planning permission from the local authority. If your application is refused unreasonably in your opinion you may want the local authority to review the application: you have the right to make a formal appeal to the Secretary of State for the Environment. Appeals must be made within six months of your application being turned down. Appeal forms can be obtained from the Secretary at the Department of the Environment.[9]

An enquiry will then be held in your area presided over by an inspector from the Department of the Environment. You have the right to appear at the enquiry and to put your side of the case. You are entitled to employ a lawyer to represent you and to call witnesses as in a Court. This procedure will not produce instant results and you will not be notified of the decision of the enquiry until some time later. A free booklet called *Planning Appeals* is available from local authority offices.

How to complain about someone else's planning scheme

If you want to complain about some proposed major planning development such as a giant superstore, a new motorway, a housing estate or an airport, there are some reasonably effective procedures for at least registering a formal complaint and if nothing else getting the authority to think again. Write as soon as possible to your local authority setting out your objections.

You may also write to the Secretary of State for the Environment,[9] formally asking for a public enquiry at which everyone's views may be heard. Ideally several people should write similar letters as a public enquiry is unlikely to be held as a result of a single complaint. A petition may be a good idea (see also page 168).

At the public enquiry you or your chosen representative will be given the opportunity to call experts and to argue why the proposed development should not go ahead. If you are a group you could together employ the services of a solicitor to present your case.

Don't consider legal action unless all else has failed.

When a planning matter reduces the value of your property

Suppose you had planned to sell your house and move into a smaller one, making a net profit. But your dreams are shattered when you learn that your present house is threatened by a compulsory purchase order, with the result either that no one is willing to buy it or that a would-be buyer is not willing to pay the price you might otherwise have expected. When a local planning decision affects the value of your property, then providing certain legal requirements are met, the house is said to be **blighted**.

By a procedure known as **service of a blight notice** you can compel the local authority to buy the property immediately for its full market value.

The procedure to take is as follows:

- contact the local planning department and ask them for the form called a **blight notice**
- complete the form and return it to the Planning Department
- compensation will be paid if the local authority accepts your claim. If it does not the case will go before a Lands Tribunal[10] whose decision is final

Where to get help

Given that there is a fairly comprehensive but complex procedure built into the law on town and country planning on how the public can complain and participate generally in planning matters, you may well feel the need for expert help and advice. The best organisation is the National Planning Aid Unit. It is a free source of:

- information about planning law and procedure
- advice on how to make use of the planning system, and how to exercise your legal rights
- contacts such as technical experts and people with experience of planning matters in your locality

Above all it will help you to help yourself. **But** it is important to realise that the National Planning Aid Unit will not fight your battles for you.

COMPLAINTS ABOUT THE POLICE

Many people believe that the police have the most difficult job of any of the public servants and recognise that in order for them to provide a safe and secure society the police have to be given special powers. But there may be a problem in the way these powers are used. For example, what of the innocent person who has been the victim of what he considers to be an abuse of police powers? What if you have reason to believe a police officer has been guilty of some dishonest or disreputable act?

What is the point in complaining?

The three main motives for making a complaint against the police are revenge, a social conscience, and the need to gather evidence for civil proceedings. The most you will achieve if your complaint is upheld is a letter of apology from the Chief Constable. One word of warning – **do not** complain lightly or frivolously. Police enquiries into complaints are time-consuming and expensive, and wasting police time is a criminal offence. Furthermore, a false and malicious complaint against an individual police officer may lead to his suing you for libel.

Making the complaint

If you do have a justified complaint go to your local police station and tell the duty officer that you would like a senior officer to take a statement from you. You will not feel popular but don't be intimidated. Alternatively, if you don't fancy this initial personal contact, write a letter outlining your grounds of complaint and send it to the Chief Constable at the police headquarters for your area. Keep a copy of the letter.

Your written complaint will be recorded, and a senior officer will be appointed to investigate it. In some cases, in order to retain a reasonable amount of impartiality, a senior officer from another force may be appointed.

The Investigating Officer is under an obligation to obtain as much evidence as he can by interviewing you first, any witnesses and then the officer or officers complained of, and to present a report to the Deputy Chief Constable, who will decide what if anything should happen next.

Where there is evidence that the officer may have broken the law, the Deputy Chief Constable[11] must report this to the Director of Public Prosecutions[12] and send him all the amassed evidence. The Director of Public Prosecutions will direct whether or not a criminal prosecution is to be brought against the officer.

There may be no evidence of law-breaking but the Deputy Chief Constable may nevertheless feel that the officer has been in breach of police disciplinary rules, and decide that a disciplinary hearing should be held.

Before the hearing takes place details of the case are sent to an independent organisation called the Police Complaints Board. It will examine the report and say whether the hearing should take the form of a formal tribunal or whether the Chief Constable himself can handle the hearing internally. The report must go to the Police Complaints Board even if the Deputy Chief Constable declares that there are no grounds for a hearing, and the Board has the authority to upturn his decision. Regardless of the form of the hearing, where the allegations are proved against the officer it is the Chief Constable of the officer's own force who decides the punishment. He can fine the officer, reduce his rank, warn him, or even dismiss him.

If you want to sue a police officer, ask at your Citizens Advice Bureau for a list of solicitors who can advise you.

As we go to press (December 1983), the police complaints system is under review.

COMPLAINTS ABOUT TRAFFIC WARDENS

Traffic wardens are hired and generally controlled by the local police force.[13] If you wish to complain about the manner in which a traffic warden is doing his job – for example swearing, or apparently exceeding his powers as you understand them – write a letter of complaint to the Chief Constable for the police force in which the traffice warden serves. The Chief Constable will then ask a police officer to investigate the complaint. The seniority of the investigating officer will be determined by the gravity of your accusations. The warden will of course be questioned as part of the investigation, and may be warned or even dismissed if the complaint is upheld.

If as a motorist you wish to complain that you should not have been given a parking ticket, take up the matter by writing to the Prosecution Officer at the address shown on the offence notice.

COMPLAINTS ABOUT EDUCATION SERVICES

The sort of complaints most commonly made about local authorities' educational services can be broken down into two identifiable categories:

■ 'in-school' complaints – for example a parent complaining about the curriculum, or that his child has been hit by a teacher
■ complaints about general educational matters – for example the admissions procedure to schools, or the threatened closure of a school

'In-school' complaints – how to deal with them

For informal complaints within the school make an appointment to see either the teacher involved in the issue or the head teacher of the school. In most cases the matter will be resolved by informal discussions.

Where in your opinion the issue has not been dealt with satisfactorily within the school, write to the Divisional Education Officer of your local authority,[14] giving details of your complaint and of the steps you have already taken to resolve it. If you are alleging incompetence or misconduct by an individual teacher, keep your letter short, factual and do not indulge in malicious or insulting comments about that teacher. The complaints procedure will vary slightly according to the nature of the complaint and the individual local authority involved.

If you are still dissatisfied after making your complaint to the LEA headquarters, you have further rights under the Education Act 1944[15] to ask the Secretary of State for Education to intervene.

87

The legal basis for your complaint is given in Sections 68 and 99 of the Act. Section 68 allows a complaint to the Secretary of State where the local education authority or a school governing body is considered to be acting 'unreasonably', and also gives the Secretary of State powers to direct the LEA to exercise its powers or perform its duties in a particular way.

In addition, Section 99 allows a complaint where the LEA is in your view failing to discharge its duties. It gives the Secretary of State powers to declare that the LEA is in default, and to give directions over the carrying out of these duties.

The section also gives the Secretary of State powers to take **mandamus** proceedings against the LEA where appropriate. This power can also be exercised by parent or guardian. Mandamus is an order from the High Court which compels the performance of public duties. To give you some idea about the scope of issues that can be brought, complaints made under these sections in the past have involved insufficient staff or equipment, inadequate maintenance of buildings, and the lack of provision for people with special educational needs.

How to complain

Your letter should be addressed to the Secretary of State for Education (for England).[16]

It should refer to Sections 68 and 99 of the Education Act 1944, and invite the Secretary of State to exercise his powers under them as a matter of urgency. Include concise details to support your complaint or refer to an appendix. If you can interest anyone else involved such as other parents or persuade a Parent/ Teacher Association to back your complaint, all the better. It is also a good idea to consult your local MP – he may take up the case on your behalf.

Complaints over general educational matters

With the exception of complaints concerning the admissions procedure and the choice of schools, the channels for complaining about general educational matters tend to be the same as those already covered. If you want to influence general educational policy in the area, your starting point is to consult and attempt to enlist the help of a councillor. The Citizens Advice Bureau and your local town hall keep names and addresses of councillors.

Whether or not a councillor will give you his support you can still make formal representations to the Divisional Education Officer, usually at local authority headquarters. If your complaint is about the way a particular policy is being interpreted, as opposed to the policy itself, the Divisional Education Officer is the most appropriate person to look into it. If you later think that he has not handled things satisfactorily, or if you feel that the matter involves unreasonable behaviour or failure by the LEA to exercise its public duties, you still have the right (in England and Wales) to complain to the Secretary of State for Education under Sections 68 and 99 of the 1944 Education Act, as previously explained.

Complaints about the choice of school

Section 6 of the Education Act 1980 (for England and Wales)[17] which came into force in September 1982 states:

Every local education authority shall make arrangements for enabling the parent of a child in the area of the authority to express a preference as to the school at which he wishes education to be provided for his child in the exercise of the authority's functions, and to give reasons for his preference.

That coupled with Section 25 of the Education Act 1944 puts LEAs under a legal obligation to heed parents' wishes over their choice of school wherever that choice is compatible with LEA resources.

Under the later Act, special local appeals tribunals have been set up to hear school choice and admissions appeals. The written appeal with full details must be sent to the Divisional Education Officer and, depending on the circumstances, may ultimately be presented before the appeals tribunal.

Ombudsman

Where you are dissatisfied with the way your local authority has handled your complaint and you think that it has caused injustice through maladministration, you have the right to ask the local government Ombudsman to investigate – see page 91 for details.

If you have complained to the Department of Education and feel they have not dealt properly with your complaint, you can take up the matter with the Parliamentary Commissioner for Administration who is the Ombudsman empowered to investigate complaints of maladministration by central government departments. Note that your complaint must be made through an MP (see page 107 for details).

Where to get help

■ **Her Majesty's Inspectorate (HMI)**
This is an officially independent body which watches over the Department of Education locally. Parents have no official and direct right of appeal, but if you send a copy of your complaint to the Inspector for your area a full inspection may be made. Through this medium, pressure may be applied in the right places.

- **The Children's Legal Centre**
  This organisation can supply information and assistance on making a formal complaint and following it up with possible legal action.
- **Advisory Centre for Education** (ACE)
  This body publishes several free leaflets on how to complain in the field of education, and will answer general queries.

COMPLAINTS ABOUT GCE EXAMINATION RESULTS

Every year hundreds of GCE candidates are dismayed by their low exam results. In both England and Wales[18] all the main examining boards have a special procedure where marks and grades can be checked, so don't let disappointment or depression deter you from appealing as soon as possible if you think you have good grounds. If you delay, the appeal may be refused.

Most boards operate three types of review.

- **A clerical check**
  This includes checking that all the necessary clerical procedures relating to a particular script have been carried out properly: have all the questions been marked? have all the marks been added up correctly?
- **Re-marking**
  The script concerned will be sent to a senior examiner who will re-mark the entire script from scratch. The results are then passed to the student's examination centre.
- **Re-marking and report**
  This involves a re-marking as described, but in addition the senior examiner draws up a report of his findings.

If you wish to take advantage of any of these procedures ask your head teacher, or the head of your exam centre, to make an application for you. In addition, he must usually give the board the reason for the appeal. The main reason for a review of some sort is where the exam result shows a marked difference from the anticipated performance. Full details of the procedures and the fees, which vary from board to board, are available from your school or from the Examining Boards Secretary.

COMPLAINTS ABOUT SOCIAL SERVICES[19]

While the Social Services Department is extremely comprehensive, demand for welfare help far exceeds the supply that can be given. This inevitably means that priorities must be fixed, with the result that some people will receive some help and others none or certainly less than they feel they need.

If you think you have been treated unfairly by the Social Services Department or are not getting the welfare help you feel entitled to write to the Director of Social Services for your area giving full details of your personal circumstances, and asking what you would like done. It may also be a good idea to seek an appointment with a local councillor who may take up the matter on your behalf. The handling of your complaint will vary from authority to authority as there is no uniform formal complaints system.

Enlist the help of some of the many organisations in the social welfare field. They will be experts on your exact entitlements and will often handle your complaint for you. Here are a few useful bodies:

- Age Concern
- Royal Association for Disability and Rehabilitation
- National Association for Mental Health (MIND)
- National Council for One Parent Families
- Gingerbread
- Child Poverty Action Group
- Shelter

If you feel that the local Social Services Department is guilty of maladministration you could refer your complaint to the local government Ombudsman (see below).

COMPLAINING TO THE LOCAL GOVERNMENT OMBUDSMAN

So far the Local Government Ombudsman has been mentioned in passing on several occasions in this section of the book. His importance is not to be underestimated. The creation of such an office in 1974 under the English Commission for Local Administration was the most important event in recent years for anyone with a complaint about a local authority.[20]

Objectives of the Commission

The objectives of the Commission are stated in their annual report. The main one is the investigation of complaints of injustice alleging maladministration by local, water and police authorities with a view to securing both satisfactory redress and better administration. The supporting objectives are:

- to encourage authorities to develop and publicise their own procedures for the fair local settlement of complaints, and to settle as many as possible
- to encourage the local settlement of complaints made to the Local Ombudsmen, although when issues of principle or public interest are involved the Local Ombudsmen may need to continue the investigation

91

- to make the Local Ombudsman system known as widely as possible and to advise people how to make their complaints
- to secure remedies quickly for those whose complaints are justified
- to make known to local government and other relevant bodies the lessons learned from investigating complaints
- to guide those with complaints outside the jurisdiction of the Local Ombudsmen
- to support the work of other Ombudsmen

When should you complain to your Local Ombudsman?

If you feel that you have been unfairly treated through a local authority's action, or indeed through its inaction, you may have grounds for complaint to your Local Government Ombudsman. Try to resolve your complaint locally first, but if you have already approached the appropriate local authority department and have asked a councillor to try to resolve your grievance, with equal lack of success, now is the time to ask the Local Ombudsman to investigate your complaint. Check first that he is empowered to do so.

What the Local Ombudsman cannot investigate

- a complaint about something that happened before April 1, 1974
- a complaint about something you knew of more than twelve months before you reported it to a Councillor (except in special circumstances)
- a complaint about which you have already gone to Court or appealed to a tribunal or a government minister
- a complaint about which you could go to a Court of Appeal (although the Local Ombudsman may investigate if he thinks it would be unreasonable to expect you to do this)
- a complaint affecting all or most of the inhabitants of a council's area, for instance a complaint that the rates have gone up

A complaint can normally only be considered by a Local Ombudsman if it is sent through a member of the local authority against which the complaint is made. Put your complaint in writing and ask a councillor to send it on to the Local Ombudsman. If he does not do so within a reasonable time you can do so yourself but tell the Local Ombudsman the name of the councillor involved.

The Local Ombudsman will examine your complaint to see whether or not he can investigate it. He may want to clear up a number of points and will contact you for this purpose, and will write to you when he has decided whether to investigate.

What form does the investigation take?

- The Local Ombudsman will ask the council for their comments.
- One of his staff may arrange to call on you and may also examine the files

of the council and interview people who have dealt with the matter. All investigations are private. The Local Ombudsman may pay your expenses, for example if you must have time off work to see his officer.

■ Some investigations are discontinued after enquiries have been made. You will be told of the reasons by letter if this is the case.

■ Other investigations continue until a formal report is issued – this will take some months. Such reports do not usually mention people's names. The report will say whether the Local Ombudsman finds that injustice has or has not been done to you by maladministration by the council. A copy will be sent to you.

How does all this help?

■ If the Local Ombudsman finds no maladministration, that is generally the end of the matter.

■ Regardless of the Local Ombudsman's findings the council complained against must make the report public by giving notice of it in the press.

■ If a report finds maladministration causing injustice, the council must tell the Local Ombudsman what it proposes to do about it.

■ Local authorities usually take steps to put right injustice. They have the power to pay to do so if necessary.

General points about complaining to Local Ombudsmen

■ Don't allow the fear of cost to put you off – the service is **free**, regardless of the outcome.

■ A free booklet about the service is available from council offices, Citizens Advice Bureaux, or direct from the Commission's office. It contains a complaint form and although it does not have to be used, all complaints must be in writing.

■ If you are not sure whether or not you should complain to him, do so – you have nothing to lose.

■ There are three Local Ombudsmen in England. Each one covers a different part of the country. For complaints about local authorities in the North and in the East Midlands approach the Local Ombudsman in York. The other two work from London (see the address section). The Scottish Ombudsman is located at Edinburgh and the Welsh one at Bridgend.

Notes: Scotland, Northern Ireland and Wales

1 In Scotland, some local authority services are provided by County, Regional or Island Councils.

In Northern Ireland, there are 27 District Councils, but their powers are relatively limited. Alongside them are various Boards (eg Education and Library Boards, Health and Social Services Boards) which work in conjunction with the relevant government departments. As usual, if you have trouble directing a complaint the Citizens Advice Bureau will help.

2 Under the Local Government (Scotland) Act 1973, local government accounts must be audited by a professional accountant appointed by the Commission for Local Authority Accounts in Scotland. Objectors to the accounts may be heard by the auditor. If he and the Accounts Commission recommend, the Secretary of State can order anyone responsible for unlawful expenditure to repay some or all of it. In Northern Ireland the corresponding Act of Parliament is the Local Government (Northern Ireland) Act 1972, and the District Auditor is called the Controller and Auditor General for Northern Ireland.

3 The Commissioner for Local Administration in Scotland and the Commissioner for Complaints are the equivalent Ombudsmen in Scotland and Northern Ireland respectively.

4 If you want to apply for a rate reduction in Scotland, contact the Assessor, the local authority official responsible for valuation for rating, who will be found at the offices of the Regional or Islands Council.

The Northern Irish office for such matters is the Rating Division of the Department of the Environment for Northern Ireland.

5 All public housing in Ulster is under the control of the Northern Ireland Housing Executive which has district offices. The Citizens Advice Bureau will help you direct the complaint.

6 The Housing (Homeless Persons) Act 1977 does not apply in Northern Ireland, but the responsibility for providing housing is with the Northern Ireland Housing Executive.

7 The corresponding Act in Scotland is the Housing (Scotland) Act 1966. There is no equivalent in Northern Ireland. Any complaints should be directed to the Public Health Officer attached to the local district council.

8 In Scotland you might also be able to take action over a housing matter under the Public Health (Scotland) Act 1897.

In Northern Ireland seek advice from the Public Health Officer before taking legal action.

9 Scotland: you have the right of appeal to the Secretary of State for Scotland; forms are available from the Scottish Development Department.

Wales: appeal forms are available from the Welsh Office.

Northern Ireland: you have the right of appeal to the Department of the Environment for Northern Ireland (Planning Division).

10 Northern Ireland has its own Lands Tribunal.

11 Complaints in Ulster may be directed to the Chief Constable of the Royal Ulster Constabulary or to the Police Authority for Northern Ireland.

12 Evidence that an officer in Scotland may have broken the law should be reported to the Procurator Fiscal.

13 Traffic wardens in Northern Ireland are employed by and accountable to the Police Authority for Northern Ireland.

14 In Northern Ireland, complaints about education services should be made first to the local Eduction and Library Board.

15 In Scotland the Education Acts do not give a specific responsibility to the Secretary of State to deal with complaints, but since he has a general responsibility for education in Scotland, complaints may be addressed to him if it is impossible for them to be resolved locally. Further, the Court of Session can compel local authorities to perform their statutory duties. However, you should seek legal advice before resorting to this remedy.

16 A letter to the equivalent of the English Secretary of State for Education should be addressed as follows:
(Scotland) The Secretary at the Scottish Education Department
(Wales) The Secretary of State for Wales
(Northern Ireland) The Minister for Education or the Commissioner for Complaints.

17 The Education (Scotland) Act 1980 has a similar provision for children to be educated in accordance with their parents' wishes, as far as possible.
    The Education (Scotland) Act 1981 allows the parent or a pupil over 16 the right to appeal when a request for a place at a specific school has been turned down. There is further right of appeal to the Sheriff beyond that, to be made within 28 days.

18 In Scotland, there is only one board, the Scottish Examination Board. As in England, it is possible to have a clerical check made, but otherwise there is no re-marking procedure at all. So if you pass, but are disappointed at the grade awarded, there is no appeal. If you fail, you may make application to the head teacher of the school, or to the principal of your further education centre. He has discretion over whether the appeal should be forwarded to the Examination Board. If he agrees, there may be a review by the Board of your work, to consider any inconsistency between school performance and the examination result. The school may be able to demonstrate that you achieved a standard higher than that shown in the exam. There is no fee charged for this service.
    For a Northern Ireland GCE candidate the thing to do is write to your school or education centre and then to the Northern Ireland Schools Examination Council.

19 In Northern Ireland, address complaints first to the local Health and Social Services Board, and only as a last resort, the Commissioner for Complaints.

20 In Scotland the creation of this office occurred in 1975. In Northern Ireland, complaints should be directed to the Commissioner for Complaints through a member of the Nothern Ireland Assembly.

Complaints about central government

Though a great many of the public services are provided and administered by local government authorities they are all ultimately answerable to a central government department. In addition to this, many services that we all take for granted are directly funded and controlled by central government offices. It would be impossible to deal here with all the complaints procedures for all the departments but this section endeavours to explain which way to complain about two of the central government departments that we all deal with at some time or another.

COMPLAINTS ABOUT THE HEALTH SERVICE

The complaints procedures outlined in this section should not be confused with complaints against doctors (GPs), dentists and pharmacists whose services are provided through local Family Practitioner Committees.[1] The way to complain about these services is dealt with on page 54. This section deals with complaints against the services provided by National Health Service hospitals and their staff. The DHSS has produced a useful leaflet called *Comments, suggestions and complaints about your stay in hospital* if you need further information. Information and advice about mental health care is available from the National Association for Mental Health (MIND).

The type of complaints made
The way in which a complaint is made and dealt with largely depends on the type of complaint. For the sake of simplicity it is possible to identify two broad categories:

- those involving the general facilities of hospitals: for example rudeness by a nurse or some other member of staff, a poorly administered appointment system resulting in a sick person being kept waiting for too long, samples for testing being mixed up
- those involving a purely medical matter – or **clinical judgement** as it tends to be called

Complain as soon as possible. A delay may weaken your argument.

Complaining about general services

Making an informal complaint

Make your complaint known to the person responsible for whatever you regard as the wrongdoing, so that things may be put right at this stage without any further aggravation or wasted time. This may not always be practical or sensible. For example, telling a nurse that you think she is incompetent and rude may seem the most tempting thing to do, but perhaps not as she is about to insert a tube up your nose. But where possible a direct complaint is the most effective method.

Making a formal complaint

If an informal complaint gets you nowhere, the next step is to put your complaint in writing to the Hospital Administrator, giving all the relevant details. The Administrator on behalf of the Area Health Authority[2] will see that a full and proper investigation is made.

The investigation itself

First of all, those against whom you are complaining will be given the opportunity to present their side of the story. If the allegations made are against a member of the medical staff and involve professional misconduct or incompetence, and it seems from early investigation that there may well be a case to answer, that person will be warned in writing that his actions, if proven, would justify serious disciplinary action. In such cases an investigatory tribunal may be set up, consisting of three independent people under the chairmanship of a legally qualified person. The person at the centre of the complaint is entitled to ask questions and call witnesses at the tribunal. The purpose of this hearing is to enable the tribunal to put together a report which is full and accurate to be sent to the Area Health Authority for their recommendations over what actions should be taken, if any.

Complaining about clinical judgement

If your complaint is about a purely medical matter, for example, if the consultant responsible for your case has with serious consequences wrongly diagnosed your illness, or has in your opinion been negligent in his treatment of your case, a specific procedure has been formulated. However, the first step is for you, a relative or a friend to ask the consultant for an appointment, and to invite him at this meeting to give you a proper explanation. Many grievances are based purely on emotional feelings and lack of knowledge on the part of the patient or his family. Or in some cases the complaint is caused by the lack of communication by the consultant. An early meeting may clear up the matter to both parties' satisfaction.

Where the matter is not resolved so happily, or your consultant seems unwilling either to meet you or give you an explanation, write to the Regional Medical Officer at the Area Health Authority[2] telling him your side of the matter and asking him to invoke the investigations procedure.

After discussions with both you and the consultant, the Regional Medical Officer will decide whether or not the matter should be taken further. If he decides that further investigation is required he will make arrangements for two independent consultants specialising in the relevant branch of medicine to consider the case in detail.

All the case notes and records will be studied and discussions held with the consultant and you the complainant. If the investigating consultants find no fault they will try to allay your anxieties. On the other hand, where the consultants feel there is some reasonable cause for grievance, a report to this effect will be made to the Regional Medical Officer. In many cases it may contain recommendations about what steps should be taken to see that a similar instance does not occur. The hospital administrator will then write to the complainant about the findings of the reviewing consultants, outlining what action has been taken in response to the investigation.

If you feel that the investigations have not been properly carried out, you can still complain to the Health Service Commissioner (the Ombudsman). See below for details.

Who can help?

- **Community Health Councils**[3] exist in each area of the country, and will often give advice and guidance if you have a genuine grievance to pursue against the health authorities. In some cases they will not merely give advice but will positively assist by representing you in the complaints and investigations procedure. Don't hesitate to get in touch with your local Community Health Council (their address is in the phone book).
- **The Patients Association** is an independent organisation offering advice to patients and representing their interests. They will answer queries on NHS or private medicine problems.
- AVMA **(Action for Victims of Medical Accidents)** may also be of help, particularly if you live in London.

The Health Service Ombudsman

If you have followed the recognised procedures for complaining against a hospital, aided perhaps by the Community Health Council,[3] but you still feel dissatisfied with the outcome either because things haven't gone your way or because you feel that the investigation has not been carried out properly, you still have one final channel which is to complain to the Health Service Commissioner – the Health Ombudsman.

The Health Ombudsman's job

It is the official function of the Health Ombudsman to investigate complaints from members of the public about injustice or hardship as a result of a health authority failing to provide a service which it was under a duty to provide, or complaints about maladministration by one of these authorities.

The Health Ombudsman cannot investigate complaints:

- which the complainant has already taken to a tribunal or Court
- about 'clinical judgement' – in other words perhaps about the diagnosis of an illness, or the treatment for that illness (this is distinct from complaining that the recognised procedure for investigating a 'clinical judgement' wasn't properly carried out)
- about GPs, pharmacists and opticians who are employed under contract by the local Family Practitioner Committee[1]
- about staff appointments and other internal workings of the health service

How to complain

There is no special form for complaining, so write to the Health Service Commissioner for the area of the United Kingdom you live in. The letter should give full details including:

- the complainant's full name and address
- the authority concerned, and the full name and address of the place where the matter complained of occurred
- a detailed account of the circumstances

It is also a good idea for you to send copies of previous correspondence with the authority about the matter at the same time.

The complaint can be made on your behalf by a friend or relative if you are unable to make it yourself. A suitable organisation may also bring the complaint. The service is free.

How your complaint will be investigated

The Health Ombudsman first has to decide whether or not your complaint is within his authority to investigate. If he feels that it is not, you will be sent a letter explaining his reasons. If he does decide that it can be investigated, he will write to you to this effect. In making his investigations the Ombudsman has power to examine the authority's records, and to interview and take written evidence from anybody thought to be of use in the investigations. He may organise an interview with you to clarify one or two points. Where this is the case you may receive any expenses incurred.

When the investigation has been completed the Ombudsman will report the result to you, to the authority complained of, and to any other appropriate bodies.

Where your allegations have been substantiated and injustice proven, the Ombudsman will propose to the relevant authority that it offers an appropriate remedy. These proposals are not instructions, merely recommendations, and the Ombudsman has no power to compel the authority to implement them, but in practice the Ombudsman's recommendations are usually heeded.

Remember, though, that legal action is the only way to get compensation. You cannot take legal action **and** seek help from the Ombudsman. If you decide to take legal action, see page 151.

COMPLAINTS ABOUT THE DEPARTMENT OF HEALTH AND SOCIAL SECURITY

The Department of Health and Social Security makes over a billion payments a year. It sends out 100 million giro cheques a year. At any given moment more than 22 million people are drawing benefits. The organisational and administrative problems of such a mammoth task are immense. Like any other organisation the DHSS does make mistakes but given the size and complexity of the job this is hardly surprising. The Department is aware that some people will have cause to complain, and the officers take seriously any reasonable complaints made in the appropriate way.

The most commonly made complaints are:

- the amount of payment made
- a delay in payment
- failure by the DHSS to supply adequate information
- complaints about the general services at a particular office, for example, queuing, rudeness by staff

Complaints about the amount of payment made

This is by far the most common complaint which the DHSS has to deal with. It is so common and potentially complex that there is a legal right to appeal that your payment is incorrect.

Supplementary benefit

Following your application for supplementary benefit, your entitlement will be calculated according to a statutory formula rather confusingly explained in a DHSS leaflet available from Post Offices and DHSS offices. The amount you are to receive, if anything, is means-tested – in other words it is dependent on your personal circumstances – and will vary a great deal between individuals. Some people are bound to feel they are not receiving what they are entitled to. You will be notified of your particular weekly entitlement, and it is now general practice within the DHSS to detail how that figure was arrived at.

If you think the amount is incorrect, your first step is to check the calculations made by the DHSS against the formula in the leaflet. The Citizens Advice Bureau or indeed your local DHSS office will be glad to help you. If you still consider the amount is wrong, proceed to the next stage.

Write to the local office saying that you think the calculations are incorrect and that you would be grateful for your application to be checked. Alternatively, invite the office to explain to you why your entitlement is less than you expected, which they will certainly do. The DHSS will only make their calculations on the figures and information you give them so **tell them everything**. It is an offence to lie about your income in order to gain money which you would otherwise not have received. On the other hand, to withhold information may mean that you are underpaid the amount of benefit due to you.

Following a further check you may still feel that you have not been given an accurate calculation of your entitlement. In these circumstances you will have a right of appeal to a special Supplementary Benefits Appeal Tribunal. You will have been told of your right to lodge an appeal in the initial letter explaining your entitlement.

If you intend to appeal you **must** do so within 28 days of the decision which you are disputing. You will only be allowed to lodge an appeal after this time if you can convince the chairman of the tribunal you had good cause for the delay. No special form is required – a letter simply stating 'I wish to appeal' with a clear account of your case will do. At this stage, if not before, seek the help of

someone with some specialised knowledge, for example the Citizens Advice Bureau.

Following this tribunal hearing there is a further right of appeal, on a point of law only, to the Social Security Commissioner.

If you feel that you have not been afforded your full rights to go through this appeals procedure, or that your complaint has been badly administered, you may complain to the Parliamentary Ombudsman. See page 107 for details.

Other Social Security benefits

While many other social benefits are dependent on National Insurance contributions such as sickness and invalidity benefit, maternity allowance, widow's pension, unemployment benefit and retirement pension, an equally large number are not dependent on contributions: heating and attendance allowances in cases of special need, for instance. If you think you have not received what you are entitled to following your applications for one or more of these benefits, the complaints procedure is almost identical to the one for supplementary benefit.

Write asking for a check to be made of your entitlement and for a full explanation. If you are not satisfied with the reply you have a right of appeal to the local National Insurance Tribunal. Again you must lodge an appeal within 28 days of the decision against which you want to appeal.

Following this there is a further right of appeal to the Social Security Commissioner. Again, where you judge that there has been some element of maladministration involved in your case, you still have recourse to the Parliamentary Ombudsman (details on page 107).

Complaints about general services at the DHSS

If you have a complaint about the general services of the DHSS you will have to rely on the Department's own internal system for resolving your complaint. For example, perhaps you agree with the amount they want to pay you but feel they are delaying in making the payment; or perhaps you have been kept queuing for an hour only to be told you were in the wrong department, or a member of staff has been rude to you. In such circumstances your first letter of complaint should be to the manager at your local DHSS office, with the envelope marked 'Personal' and the letter headed 'Letter of Complaint'. Always give him the opportunity of trying to resolve your dispute before you proceed further. Whether he looks into the matter and supervises any investigation himself largely depends on the seriousness of the complaint. If it involves an allegation of serious misconduct, the person accused will probably be consulted by the manager in order to hear the other side of the story. You are also likely to be visited by an officer from the department for further details.

Following these investigations a letter of explanation will be sent to you, outlining what the investigations have discovered, and offering an apology if your complaint was found to be substantiated.

If you are not satisfied with the outcome you could still write to the local manager's superior, the Regional Controller,[4] asking him to look into the matter.

If you feel that your complaint has still not been properly treated, particularly where you feel there has been maladministration causing injustice or hardship, you could bring your complaint to the notice of your Member of Parliament, who may take the matter up on your behalf. He may also be of help if you wish to complain about the Social Security system itself. You may feel that the law needs changing on a particular issue, and consulting your MP is the best way to raise the matter in the right place, namely in Parliament.

There is no reason why after all this you shouldn't write to the Minister asking him to look into the matter.

The final place to raise your complaint if all else has failed is with the Parliamentary Ombudsman, who will look into allegations of maladministration by central government. Full details of this are on page 107.

COMPLAINTS ABOUT TAX

Many complaints against central government are about the way in which money is spent. This section deals with complaints about the way that money is raised. The main method of raising money is through taxation in various forms: Capital Gains Tax, Corporation Tax, Capital Transfer Tax, Income Tax, Value Added Tax – it seems whichever way we turn there is some tax or other.

The purpose of this section is to give guidance on procedures for complaining about tax matters, and what might be gained from such actions. There is a well-regulated system for registering complaints or disputes in order that they can be investigated and put right where necessary. For the purposes of simplicity VAT will be looked at later on in the section (page 105) as there is a special appeals system for it.

Complaining about your tax coding

If you are employed, income tax will usually be automatically deducted from your pay through the Pay as You Earn scheme (PAYE). If you are on this scheme, you will receive from time to time **a notice of coding** which sets out the allowances you can claim against tax. It is on the basis of this coding that deductions of a particular amount will be made from your say.

On receiving your Notice of Coding you should check it to see that you have got the correct code. Either get professional help on this, or consult for example the March edition of *Which?* magazine for its annual *Tax-Saving Guide.*

If you feel the code is still incorrect, write to your tax inspector asking him to change it. It may be a perfectly innocent mistake, for example your circumstances may have changed during the year and the tax man doesn't know because you haven't told him. If you get no satisfaction from writing to your tax inspector in this way, you have a right of appeal to the General Commissioner (see below).

Complaining about your tax assessment

If you think that the Inland Revenue has asked you to pay more tax than you are liable for, you have **a right to appeal against your tax assessment**. You cannot appeal merely because you object to having to pay so much out of your income in tax. You can seek help in checking the assessment from an accountant (if you are self-employed such a person is strongly advisable), or from the Citizens Advice Bureau, or again you may be able to use the Consumers' Association's *Tax-Saving Guide*.

How to appeal

The same right of appeal exists whether you have a complaint about PAYE or some other type of tax, such as Capital Gains, Transfer Tax, or Corporation Tax (but not VAT – see opposite). You need to obtain the Appeal Form 64-7 from your local tax office. It is also advisable to ask there for leaflet IR 37 on Income Tax and Capital Gains Tax Appeals.

You should send the completed form to your Tax Inspector within thirty days of the date of the initial assessment. Occasionally if you have a good reason the Inland Revenue will permit you to make an appeal outside the 30-day period. An illness, for example, might be the sort of circumstances when such an extension would be allowed.

Your Tax Inspector will review your case and notify you of his decision. If you are not satisfied with his decision, you can proceed to the next stage of the complaints procedure, by appealing to the Special or General Commissioner. Very often you can choose which you would like to hear your appeal. **Special Commissioners** are appointed by the Treasury and are full-time specialists expert in tax matters. **General Commissioners** are laymen and form the panel at a local hearing. Unless your appeal is based on a technical rule of law, you should choose to take your case to the General Commissioners, who deal with cases in a quicker and cheaper way.

At the hearing evidence will be presented, documents produced, witnesses called and questioned. Where the decision taken by the Commissioner is based

---

Don't be afraid to seek expert advice when you feel you can't handle the situation yourself.

---

on a point of law, you have the legal right to appeal to the High Court. But no appeal is allowed when the decision of the Commissioner is based on a point of fact. You have the right to be represented before the Commissioner by a professional person, and it is often wise to take advantage of this right. Legal aid is not available for appeals before the Commissioners – you must bear the costs of the appeal yourself even if you win.

Complaints about tax management

If you have a complaint about the way in which the tax system is being applied, or if you have been treated discourteously, you should take the matter up with the District Inspector in the case of tax offices, or the Collector in Charge in the case of collection offices. These people have the day-to-day responsibility for the work of their staff and should be able to give your complaint prompt and proper attention.

If you are dissatisfied with an investigation by or on behalf of a District Inspector or Collector in Charge, it would be appropriate to write to the Inland Revenue's regional office to which these officials are directly answerable.

Ultimately, of course, if you are still dissatisfied with the way the matter has been looked at, or if you feel that somewhere along the lines there has been maladministration, you might consider referring your complaint to the Parliamentary Ombudsman through your MP (see page 107 for details).

Complaints about VAT

Unlike the other kinds of taxes already mentioned, Value Added Tax (VAT) is under the care and management of the Department of Customs and Excise, as opposed to the Inland Revenue, so it is to Customs and Excise then you must take your complaint. Complaints about VAT tend to fall into two categories:

- complaints by consumers about the way in which a particular trader is administering the VAT system, for example if VAT has been charged inappropriately
- complaints by a trader against Customs and Excise over a number of problems, for example over the registration for VAT, or the amount paid or said to be payable

Consumers' complaints

As a consumer you may feel aggrieved at the way a trader has dealt with you: for example you have been charged VAT when you believe, given the deal or kind of supplies or services provided, that no VAT should be payable.

This is not really a matter for the Customs and Excise but for you and the trader to resolve. If you do want to take the matter further, contact the local VAT office who will advise you on the rights and wrongs of the trader's behaviour to you. Once you are certain that the system has been wrongly applied in your case you should approach the trader armed with your new information. If he will not accept what you say, report him to Customs and Excise who will advise him.

If you believe the trader was deliberately abusing the system for his own personal gain report him to the Trading Standards Department[5] who will investigate and possibly prosecute.

Traders' complaints

On the whole it is really only the business fraternity who have justifiable cause to complain over VAT. There is a special Value Added Tax tribunal to which individual traders can appeal when they are unable to reach a satisfactory resolution of the complaint by dealing with local VAT officers.

Common examples of things you can appeal against to the tribunal

■ the registration or cancellation of the registration of yourself as a taxable person
■ an assessment of how much VAT you should pay to Customs and Excise
■ the tax which is chargeable on the supply of goods or services

There are many other grounds for an appeal to the tribunal – too numerous to list fully here – but the local VAT office will supply you with a comprehensive leaflet on the tribunal. They will also be able to advise you about the procedure for applying to take your case before a tribunal.

How to appeal
Set out all the relevant facts and information and ask the VAT officer dealing with your case to review the matter again. This is certainly preferable to a formal tribunal hearing and is always worth a try. Note that any application for an appeal to the tribunal should be made within thirty days after you have heard the decision of the Customs and Excise, so you should lodge your appeal immediately and not wait until your case has been reviewed again.

An appeal is set in motion by completion of a **Notice of Appeal** (Form Trib 1) which is available from any VAT office.

In order for the tribunal to entertain your appeal all the VAT returns required

---

A raised number denotes that the complaints procedure differs in Scotland or Northern Ireland – see the end of the chapter.

---

must have been completed in accordance with the regulations, and the amount determined by Customs and Excise as payable as tax must have been paid or deposited with them. Special permission for this latter condition to be waived may be given where the person making the appeal (the appellant) can show he would suffer hardship.

The hearing

A number of procedural events take place: the department drafts a statement of their case, a copy of which is sent to you; a list of all the documents to be exchanged at the hearing is put together; witness statements are made. You must be given not less than 14 days' notice of the date, time and place of the appeal. You can be represented at the hearing by anyone.

The Chairman of the tribunal may announce the decision at the end of the hearing, but in any event a written document containing all the findings of fact and the tribunal's reason for the decision will be sent to you or the person acting on your behalf. An appeal against a decision at a Value Added Tax tribunal can be made to the High Court of Justice, but note that there is only a right of appeal on a point of law. Where a tribunal decides that any tax paid or deposited should be repaid, interest can also be recovered.

COMPLAINING TO THE PARLIAMENTARY OMBUDSMAN

Where you are alleging maladministration against a central government department and you have attempted to resolve the matter through all the other available complaints procedures, then as a last resort you have the right to complain to the Parliamentary Ombudsman.

The Ombudsman's role is to investigate complaints referred to him by MPs on behalf of members of the public who feel they have suffered injustice because of maladministration by any one of many government departments.

How to complain

If you have a complaint which you want the Ombudsman to investigate your first step is to see your MP who may look into the matter on your behalf and resolve it successfully himself. Thus you are provided with an additional channel for your complaint en route to the Parliamentary Ombudsman. All MPs hold regular surgery for their constituents (the Citizens Advice Bureau will be able to tell you when and where). If your own MP will not help you you must enlist the help of another. The Ombudsman has no power of investigation unless the matter is referred to him through an MP. If the MP is willing to pass it on to the Ombudsman, either straightaway or after he has attempted to resolve it for you, you should put your complaint in writing to the MP, including:

- your name and address
- the identity of the department against whose action the complaint is made
- a statement of the circumstances in which you the complainant claim to have sustained injustice
- a statement that you give your consent for the complaint to be referred to the Ombudsman

You must make your complaint to the MP within 12 months of the circumstances leading to your complaint coming to light. You can't use the Ombudsman's services if you have already exercised a right of appeal to a Court or tribunal, or could have done so. Your complaint may be made by you or someone acting on your behalf.

The investigation procedure

The investigation procedure falls into three parts:

- **the preliminary examination** by the Ombudsman to determine whether the case is within his authority to investigate
- **the investigation** which will be full and thorough. The Ombudsman has wide-ranging powers to obtain information which he believes to be relevant. He can obtain access to Ministerial and Departmental documents which would normally be private. He can take written and oral evidence from anyone he believes is concerned. An officer from his Office may visit you to clear up any additional points. You may even be asked to appear in person for an interview (you will be entitled to expenses for such a visit)
- **the report** on the case which will be sent to the MP through whom the complaint was initially referred. A copy of this report is presented to Parliament. If the Ombudsman finds that injustice has been sustained he can, and often does, propose to the appropriate department that they offer a suitable remedy

Notes: Scotland and Northern Ireland

1 Area Health Boards are the Scottish equivalent of the English Family Practitioner Committees.

2 The Area Health Boards in Scotland also hold the responsibility of the Area Health Authorities in England and Wales.

3 Community Health Councils: the Scottish equivalents are the Local Health Councils; in Northern Ireland the work is done by the Central Services Agency.

4 The Scottish counterpart of the Regional Controller is the Controller.

5 In Northern Ireland the role of Trading Standards Department is played by the Trading Standards Branch of the Department of Economic Development for Northern Ireland.

Complaints about business institutions

COMPLAINTS ABOUT INSURANCE

Most of us go through life believing 'it can't happen to me!' 'It' can be any number of mishaps from such domestic catastrophes as a burst pipe, to a serious car accident. Despite this, most of us cover ourselves against these eventualities and spend millions of pounds a year on insurance. The basis of any insurance policy is that you, the insured, enter into a contract with the insurer whereby, in return for your paying an agreed sum of money (the premium) they agree to take on the risk of having to make good any loss you suffer through certain specified 'perils' such as fire, theft or damage. It sounds simple enough but in practice these contracts are so complex, and to the layman so full of legal mumbo jumbo, that complaints and disputes inevitably arise. It is possible to insure just about anything from cancellation of an event because of the weather to a specific part of your anatomy, but the most usual things people insure are:

- their life
- their house and its contents
- their car

Unlike many industries and groups there is not merely one body to whom you can complain or one complaints procedure. Which organisation you go to and the procedure to follow will vary according to the kind of insurance policy. For the sake of simplicity a distinction will be made between the following two types of insurance.

- general insurance – motor, house and contents, travel, personal accident insurance – in fact, all non-life insurance matter
- life insurance

If it is your insurance broker rather than your policy or claim that you want to complain about, see page 63.

Don't sign anything without reading it first. If you don't understand what you're signing ask for an explanation.

General insurance

If you have a complaint about some aspect of a general insurance policy (a non-life policy), refer the matter to the manager of the branch or office of the insurance company where the policy was issued. If you do not know which office issued the policy, write to the head office.

If this does not resolve the matter satisfactorily, put the issue, again in writing, to the Chief Executive at the company's head office (the address will be on the policy document or renewal notice).

If neither move gets you anywhere, send full details of your policy, complaint and previous correspondence to the British Insurance Association's Consumer Information Department. This department was set up to deal amongst other things with complaints against member companies. Under this service the British Insurance Association (BIA) refers complaints to the senior management of the member company concerned to ensure that the complaint is investigated and fully considered. No approach is made by the BIA to the branch office involved in the complaint. After a full investigation, and depending of course on the circumstances, a member company may decide to conduct further negotiations itself in an attempt to achieve an amicable settlement with the complainant, or it may well maintain its original decision on the case. This further investigation by the BIA may also reveal some new information or, as often happens, simply rectify a previous lack of communication.

The BIA deals with about 2,600 complaints every year, but its limitations are that it cannot automatically:

- provide an arbitration service between the disputing parties
- compel a member company to adopt a particular method of doing business
- negotiate a claim on behalf of the complainant
- deal with complaints about companies which are not members of BIA

If you are not sure whether a particular company is a member of the BIA or not, or indeed if you are aware that it is not but don't know of a professional association it does belong to, you should still send in details of your complaint to the BIA. After a basic acknowledgement they will pass on your correspondence to the appropriate body, for example the Advisory Division at Lloyds if it is a Lloyds policy, or to the British Insurance Brokers' Association if your policy was arranged through an insurance broker. In some cases the BIA will refer you to the Insurance Ombudsman Bureau (more details on page 112).

If you are unhappy with the way the BIA has handled your complaint, or although satisfied with their handling of the issue you are still not happy with the ultimate outcome, you can refer your complaint to the Insurance Ombudsman Bureau or a service operated by the Chartered Institute of Arbitrators (see page 113).

In some cases if you remain dissatisfied you can still go to Court over the matter but not if you have involved the Chartered Institute of Arbitrators. Seek professional advice first.

Life insurance

To a certain degree the various steps in the complaints procedure for life insurance policies are the same as with non-life policies, but the organisations who can help differ.

Take up the matter with the local office or a local representative of the life insurance company. If that gets you nowhere write to the head office of the company. Give as many details as possible: your policy number, the basis of your complaint, and any correspondence or documents relating to your complaint.

If the complaint remains unresolved, the most appropriate organisation to write to is the Life Offices Association in London or the Associated Scottish Life Offices in Edinburgh.

For Industrial Life or Linked Life policies write to the Industrial Life Offices Association or the Linked Life Assurance Group, both in London.

Complaints over life policies issued by members of the BIA which are not members of those associations mentioned above should still be directed to the BIA. Complaints about life policies underwritten by Lloyds should be directed to their Advisory Department.

Each of these associations and organisations maintains a full-time complaints and information service. Most complaints arise from a breakdown of communications or an administrative failure and are usually rectified once the issue is directed to the right quarters.

Additionally, with industrial life policies only, a Government official, the Industrial Assurance Commissioner, is available to deal with disputes and complaints and has powers to adjudicate in disputes. His address is contained in every policyholder premium receipt book. Sometimes a small fee is payable if a hearing is involved.

In the unlikely event that none of these groups is able to resolve matters satisfactorily, certain aspects of life policies can be considered by the Insurance Ombudsman (industrial life policies are specifically included) but only after a senior manager of the company concerned has been consulted. Some matters can be referred to the Chartered Institute of Arbitrators. (More details on both these schemes overleaf.)

If one of the trade associations or Lloyds has failed to resolve a complaint you could ask the Insurance Division at the Department of Trade to look into your complaint particularly where alleged malpractice or financial instability is concerned. You could also bring in the Insurance Division much earlier if the complaint involves an insurer who is not a member of a trade association or Lloyds.

If all these methods of resolving your dispute fail your final recourse is to take legal action in the Courts. Apart from the scheme run by the Institute of Arbitrators, none of the other methods prejudices your rights to take legal action. Make sure you obtain professional and specialist advice.

The Insurance Ombudsman

The appointment of the Insurance Ombudsman (watchdog) and the establishment of the Insurance Ombudsman Bureau (IOB) in 1981 came about because a number of insurance companies felt that there was a distinct need for an independent, informal, well-publicised and free procedure for dissatisfied policyholders to deal with their complaints. There is no charge for the Insurance Ombudsman's services: the work of the IOB is paid for by the insurance companies in the scheme. They want to protect their reputations by making sure that none of their customers feels unfairly treated.

What kind of disputes does the Insurance Ombudsman deal with?
He can only attempt to settle your dispute if the insurance company you are complaining against is in the Insurance Ombudsman Scheme (find out by asking the company, the Ombudsman, or the Citizens Advice Bureau). Here are a number of examples of complaints the Insurance Ombudsman might deal with:

- As a motorist you may be in dispute with your insurance company over your no claims bonus or a third party claim.
- After a fire at your home you may think that the payment offered you is too small.
- You may be unhappy about the payment offered for baggage lost on holiday.

The Insurance Ombudsman cannot deal with 'Industrial Life' policies or other life insurance disputes such as the value of a policy when cashed in early. Check that your complaint about life insurance is one within the Ombudsman's powers – he is the best person to check with.

How to make a complaint to the Insurance Ombudsman
Before a policyholder can take a complaint to the Ombudsman all normal channels of negotiation with the member company must have been exhausted. This means that the complaint must have been considered both by the branch and senior management of the company in question. It is also important to note that a decision to use the Insurance Ombudsman must be taken within six months of learning of the company's final decision.

Using the scheme does not preclude the policyholder from resorting to legal action if he rejects the Insurance Ombudsman's decision.

There is no formal application form. Send a short letter to the Insurance

Ombudsman Bureau explaining the nature of your complaint, and include the name of the insurance company you are complaining about, and your policy number. Don't send the policy yet. If the Ombudsman can deal with your dispute he will let you know.

The Insurance Ombudsman will study your letter and check if it is within his authority to deal with the case. If it is he may require further details from you, and he has the power to see all the company's papers about your case. He may call in expert advice, and you may be asked to go to a hearing. He may try to settle the dispute by giving advice or by bringing together the two sides. If not, he will make a decision, which may amount to a recommendation one way or the other, or which may be a cash award in your favour. All member companies have agreed to abide by the Insurance Ombudsman's findings up to an award of £100,000. In very simplified terms he will make a sensible and fair decision based on the law and good insurance practice.

What happens after a decision depends on you more than anything else. The Ombudsman will send his decision to you and to the insurance company. You can accept or reject the decision. If you accept it the company must pay you any award up to £100,000 and must also look carefully at any recommendations made by the Ombudsman. If you reject it, the decision is cancelled. You are then free to do as you wish. If you want to take legal action your legal rights will not have been changed by the Ombudsman's decision.

The Chartered Institute of Arbitrators – Personal Insurance Arbitration Service

A number of insurance companies who were not part of the Ombudsman scheme decided in response to look into the merits of coming up with an alternative aimed at achieving a similar objective. Their investigations came upon a service operated by the Chartered Institute of Arbitration already functioning in a number of trades and industries and approved by the Office of Fair Trading, which would also be appropriate to the insurance industry. The main features of the service are that:

- it is available to personal insurance policyholders after disputes remain unresolved despite consideration at the most senior level of the insurance company concerned
- the arbitration decision is binding on both parties
- there is no charge for the service

Give the person or body you are complaining about a chance to voice their side of the case and to put things right first. This will probably save everyone a lot of wasted time and aggravation.

COMPLAINTS ABOUT BANKS

As in every other business, banks inevitably give rise to complaint from time to time. What is perhaps surprising, though, is that there is no 'watchdog' body or general association to lay down codes of practice and behaviour to which the banks must adhere, and also no uniform procedure exists within the different banks for dealing with complaints. However, if you do have a complaint against one of the leading banks here are some general suggestions for getting it rectified.

Approach the person you dealt with. The majority of complaints tend to be about some genuine human error or some basic misunderstanding which can be cleared up immediately.

If this does not prove successful, write to the manager of the branch or department involved. Give full details of your complaint and say what you would like them to do about it. Keep a copy of the letter. In most cases, if your complaint is justified, the manager should be able to put matters to rights.

If you are still dissatisfied with the action taken by the manager or more generally with the way your complaint has been dealt with, go on up the ladder to the Area Director of the bank. Most leading banks have such officials and his address can be obtained from any branch. Send him details of your complaint, enclosing copies of all previous correspondence. If the complaint involves one of the bank's departments write to the Head or Principal of that department.

If you are still unhappy, take the matter up with the head office. Write either to the Head of Public Relations, or to the Chairman of the bank.

The Banking Information Service has no arbitration powers but may help you by taking an objective view of any dispute and advise on standard banking practices.

Most complaints are resolved one way or the other before there is any need to complain to the head office. Don't forget that you hold the ultimate weapon: you can simply open an account with another bank. Remember that they need you as much, and sometimes more, than you need them.

How the law can help

In some circumstances your complaint might not just involve some grievance against the general standard of service offered by a bank, but you may feel that there has been a serious infringement of your basic legal rights. Where this is the case, legal action against the bank becomes a further possibility if they will not settle the matter amicably. For example, the bank is under a legal obligation not to pass on confidential information about a customer without proper authority (other than in a few exceptional cases); it must honour a customer's cheques up to whatever amount has been agreed by way of an overdraft and it would be liable to bear the loss if it paid out on cheque or a banker's card which you had told them was lost or stolen. Seek expert advice before you enter into legal wranglings with a bank.

COMPLAINTS ABOUT BUILDING SOCIETIES

Over fifty per cent of the adult population have savings with building societies, and the various societies between them have over five and half million borrowers. Given these figures, it is hardly surprising that some people will have a complaint from time to time, although it must be said that the number of complaints is relatively small.

If you feel you have a genuine complaint against a building society the steps to take are as follows.

Write to the Manager of the branch of the society involved. Explain the basis of your complaint and tell him what you would like him to do about it. More often than not a complaint is either about a fairly simple administrative matter, or about a breakdown of communications. In any event, the Manager will usually be able to put things right if the society has been at fault, or at least offer you an acceptable explanation.

If you feel this is inadequate send all the relevant details to the head office of

115

the society. Building societies in general are very conscious of their public image, and will treat justified complaints seriously.

Your final course of action is to complain to the Building Societies Association, but always attempt to resolve the matter yourself by writing to the head office of the building society involved before complaining to the Building Societies Association, and also make your complaint in writing, as a telephoned complaint will usually not be acted upon.

Where a complaint appears on the face of it to have some justification, or where it seems clear that a particular society is acting against certain of the Association's recommendations, a copy of the complaint will be sent to the Chief Executive of the society involved inviting his comments. When the Association has a full picture of the facts, you will be advised of your position and whether the society has been recommended to rectify matters. However, the Building Societies Association is not a 'complaints bureau', and has no powers to compel an individual society to adopt a particular line of action.

Ultimately you can always take your business elsewhere. There are over 200 building societies, as well as banks and other financial institutions which keeps the societies responsive to consumer needs.

Complaints about neighbours

Frequent all-night parties next door, constant pleas by a neighbour's seven-year-old who 'wants his ball back', a neighbour with a fetish for lighting bonfires every other night. Do any of these sound familiar? Disputes with neighbours tend to bring out the worst in people who are normally quite placid.

It is generally recognised that in order to live a reasonably peaceful and civilised life we have to put up with a certain degree of noise, smell and general inconvenience caused by others, but occasionally complaining seems necessary. This section will explain the legal side of such complaints and what sort of action you might take.

One thinks of neighbours as the people literally next door, but the law gives the word a much wider meaning, and it is in this context that the term is used in this section of the book. So a neighbour is anyone directly affected by what you do at home to the extent that you should give them some consideration, and vice versa of course.

NUISANCES

As far as the law is concerned, there are two main categories of nuisance: **private** and **public**. The way in which you complain will depend on which of these two is involved.

Private nuisance

It is impossible to list all the various nuisances that may amount in law to private nuisance, but excessive noise, smell, inconvenience are all included. The essence of private nuisance, if you are to have any legal remedy over the matter, is that you must be able to establish that your neighbour is not merely noisy or smelly but that what he is doing has some element of **continuity** about it and that it is **interfering with the enjoyment of your property**.

Private nuisance is a purely civil matter: if you feel so aggrieved about the 'nuisance' that you want to seek some remedy, you alone must do so as one individual against the person responsible for causing the nuisance.

Public nuisance

A public nuisance is one that affects the public at large, as opposed to one specific person: a vehicle blocking the public highway, and industrial premises continually emitting toxic fumes, are public nuisances. Some public nuisances are declared to be such by virtue of some Act of Parliament, or by some bye-law, such as one stating where rubbish should not be tipped. In general, public nuisance is a crime, and the responsibility and expense of taking action will not be yours but that of the local authority. However, if a public nuisance is causing particular inconvenience to one person, that person may still bring a civil action.

What to do about a nuisance

The first step is to discover what kind of nuisance is involved, private or public. If you think it may be a **public nuisance**, check with the local authority whether any statutory or bye-law nuisance has been committed. The Environmental Health Officer, whose address and phone number will be listed in your local telephone directory under the local District Council, is usually the person to contact. If a public nuisance has been committed the authorities will normally serve an **abatement notice** on the offender requiring him to put a stop to whatever the nuisance is. Failure to adhere to this notice could mean a fine.

If you discover that the nuisance is a purely **private nuisance** then you must resolve the matter yourself. Talk to the person responsible, explaining your position. It is surprising how many people let things get out of hand before taking this basic step. If it doesn't work, write a polite but formal letter to the person asking him to stop causing the nuisance and informing him that unless he does as you ask you will commence legal proceedings.

If you do not get a satisfactory response to this letter, legal action is unfortunately the only answer. You must decide whether you simply want to get the person to stop causing the nuisance altogether, or whether in addition you want to claim compensation. Usually if you want to claim compensation you will have to show that the nuisance has caused some specific damage or loss: for example, the noise next door has prevented you sleeping thus affecting your health, or the vibrations from your neighbour's engineering equipment have caused structural damage to your property. At this stage you should seek the professional advice of a solicitor or get help from a competent person or body such as the Citizens Advice Bureau.

Remember, take legal action as the last resort after all peaceful attempts to resolve the matter have failed. Court action can be expensive and often inconclusive, and of course it doesn't do a great deal for future neighbourly relations.

Noise

Where a noise is unreasonable, whether a neighbour's hi-fi or barking dog, you can report the nuisance to the Environmental Health Officer at the Town Hall.[1]

Complaints about aircraft noise should be addressed to the Civil Aviation Policy Division (5B) at the Department of Trade. You might also consider lobbying your MP with a view to getting flight paths changed.

TRESPASS

Someone is trespassing on your property if he is on it without your permission. However, that permission may be implied, so you have no grounds to complain that the milkman or the postman is trespassing because he has implied consent to be on your property, but only for the purposes of delivering the milk or the mail. If he wanders into your back garden to admire the roses he becomes a trespasser. If you believe that someone is a trespasser, you can take one of three courses of action:

- Invite the trespasser to leave, informing him that you regard him as a trespasser. Even if someone is not trespassing when they come on to the

119

land, once you withdraw your permission for him to remain, a trespass is committed.

- You can use **reasonable force** to get a trespasser to leave your property. How much force is reasonable is obviously difficult to say. For example, you would be entitled to use a greater amount of force to remove an armed thief than a small child who has come into your garden to retrieve his football. If you use too much force you can be guilty of a criminal offence and you may also be liable for compensation to the person on whom you used excessive force. The same applies if you deliberately intend to injure a trespasser by setting traps, and you may even be liable if they are injured by falling over while trespassing.

- You can take legal action against a trespasser to recover compensation where damage has been caused. In fact even if no specific damage has been caused by the trespasser you can still recover a small amount of damages simply as an acknowledgement that your legal rights have been infringed. Again legal action should really only be considered where the trespass is a fairly serious matter and other attempts to resolve the issue have failed.

DISPUTES OVER BOUNDARIES AND FENCES

Arguments between neighbours over who owns what, where the boundary is between the two properties, whose responsibility is it to maintain fences – such problems are unfortunately all too common. The only way to resolve them is by discovering who in fact owns what and where the responsibility lies. Here are a few suggestions and general guidelines to enable you to find out.

The **title deeds** to the property will sometimes, though not always, clarify the matter. If your property is mortgaged, the building society or the bank will be holding the title deeds. You should write and tell them you would like to inspect them, and ask for them to be made available for your inspection. This may take place at the office of a solicitor of their choosing. The title deeds may mention a particular person's responsibility to look after such and such a fence, or may specify who owns what; sometimes a plan will be included showing who owns which fence. Your dispute may end up as a draw, as sometimes fences are declared party fences, in other words, shared.

Where the deeds are of no help the fence itself may be of some guidance: as a general rule (although again it does not always follow) the fence will be owned by the person living on the side of the fence posts.

Where none of these steps ends the matter and the dispute becomes serious, legal action may be the only way to get a declaration on who owns what. Don't forget that the Court can only make a decision on all the surrounding circumstances and the evidence presented by both parties.

COMPLAINTS ABOUT TREES

Your answer to overhanging branches and undermining roots is simple – cut them off. Yes, you have the right to do this, but before you get finger-happy with your garden tools, do the decent thing first and invite your neighbour on to your land to cut off the branches or roots himself. The end product is the same, but the courtesy may well save a complaint from your neighbour who does not know the law, and therefore does not realise that you were quite within your rights to give his tree the chop.

Where he has refused to cut the tree himself and you have exercised your right to trim the growth back to the boundary line, your only further obligation is to offer the pieces back to the owner. As far as fruit trees are concerned the same rules apply and your neighbour is also entitled to the fruit from his tree.

COMPLAINTS ABOUT DOGS

You may well have justifiable cause to complain about the behaviour of dogs barking late at night, fouling the footpath or your garden, frightening your children. There are several legal obligations[2] imposed on dog owners over the extent that they control their animals, and a number of remedies which a complainant may make use of.

Fouling the footpath[3]

In many areas, local authority bye-laws make it a criminal offence for a dog owner to permit his animal to foul the footpath. If you wish to see that someone is prosecuted for this offence inform the local authority or the police. If you wish to instigate the prosecution yourself, perhaps because the authorities are unwilling to do so, you have the right. First check with the local authority exactly which bye-law has been infringed by the dog owner. Then go to your local Magistrates Court Office and say you want to take out a private prosecution against the owner for allowing his dog to foul the footpath under such and such a bye-law. Note that the dog owner can usually escape conviction if he can show that he made reasonable attempts to take the animal to the road or gutter, or even the grass verge in some cases. Also realise that a prosecution resulting in a conviction will only bring about a punishment for the dog owner and will not bring you any compensation. If the dog fouled your garden, and you can show that the dog owner did nothing to prevent the dog doing so, you can sue him for trespass and claim compensation.

Noisy dogs

The local authority may also have established bye-laws which prohibit dogs being unreasonably noisy in a particular area. The local authority may prosecute in such circumstances but again you may be left to bring a private prosecution yourself. Before doing so, give the dog owner reasonable opportunity of quietening the dog.

If you get nowhere by asking the owner to keep his dog quiet, you should serve a **formal notice** on the owner specifying a time limit within which he must rectify the problem. The notice must be signed by at least three other affected householders and should be sent by recorded delivery.

Dangerous dogs[4]

If you regard a particular dog as dangerous, and believe that it is not being, or has not been, properly controlled or supervised, the owner can be prosecuted under the Dogs Act 1871. The local authority can prosecute and should be urged to do so. After all, if the dog is genuinely dangerous and is not being controlled satisfactorily, it is in the general public's interest that something be done.

If the authorities refuse, you still have the right to bring a private prosecution. The procedure is as before: tell the local Magistrates Court that you want to take out a private prosecution and give all the details. In practice it is not always easy to establish that the dog is as dangerous as you allege. Sometimes, before convicting, the Magistrates require evidence that the dog has caused a danger to someone on another occasion, apart from the one for which you are bringing the prosecution. The sort of things that might lead to a successful prosecution, however, are a dog attacking or chasing someone, snapping and frightening children, or worrying sheep. The Magistrate can order that the owner keep the dog under control and in serious cases he can order that the dog be destroyed.

Notes: Scotland and Northern Ireland

1 In Northern Ireland the Environmental Health Officer is usually found at the local district council office.

2 Northern Irish dogs are regulated by the Dogs (Northern Ireland) Order 1983. Any complaints should be directed to the Local District Council which has the power to make the owners comply.

3 In Scotland, the Civic Government (Scotland) Act 1982 makes it a criminal offence to allow a dog to foul a footpath, grass verge, pedestrian precinct, children's play area or other open space designated by the local authority. Prosecution is by the Procurator Fiscal (there is virtually no private prosecution in Scotland).

4 The same Act deals with dangerous dogs in Scotland, but the animal cannot be destroyed.

Disputes between private landlords and tenants

The law which regulates the way landlords and tenants behave or should behave towards each other is extremely complicated. Numerous Acts of Parliament and legal rules exist specifically to deal with this area. Therefore whether you are a landlord or a tenant the key to your success in any dispute is knowing your basic legal rights. There are a number of organisations and places where you can get help and advice.

- Several free leaflets on the subject issued by the Department of the Environment provide a very useful summary of the law relating to landlords and tenants. They are available from any Citizens Advice Bureau.
- You can also seek personal advice from the Citizens Advice Bureau, or from a Housing Aid and Advice Centre[1] in your town or city. Shelter may also be able to answer specific queries.

There are two different forms of landlord and tenant relationships:

- **public sector tenancies** where the landlord is the local council and the tenant is living in a council house
- **private sector tenancies** where the landlord is an individual

This section of the book deals **only** with private sector tenancies. Problems to do with council house tenancies are covered in the Local Government section on page 80.

COMPLAINTS BY TENANTS ABOUT LANDLORDS

These are the most common complaints tenants have about their landlords, whether in furnished or unfurnished properties. The list is not exhaustive, but it represents both the most common and important complaints:

- the rent is too high
- the landlord has told the tenant to leave without proper cause or notice
- the landlord is not maintaining and repairing the property as he should
- the landlord is harassing the tenant

The way that you as a tenant should act if you have a grievance depends on your complaint, and on where you stand in the eyes of the law.

The rent is too high

If you genuinely consider that the rent is too high, given the facilities (not merely that you don't like paying so much), or if indeed the landlord decides to put up the rent once you have moved in, there is a statutory system by which you can complain and have the matter looked at impartially. The system is known as the **registration of a fair rent.**

The right to apply for the registration of a fair rent on the whole only applies to a tenant in what is called a **regulated tenancy**, that is, the letting of all or part of a house, flat, maisonnette or bungalow, either furnished or unfurnished, providing:

- the landlord does not live in the same property
- the landlord is not a local authority or a housing association (although housing authorities have a similar system)
- the landlord is not a government department
- the landlord is not a university, college or polytechnic letting to one of its students
- the let is not a holiday let
- there is no board

The landlord of a regulated tenancy also has the right to apply for the registration of a fair rent (more on this below).

How does a tenant apply for a fair rent to be registered?

You must complete the appropriate application form which the Rent Officer will provide (he is listed in the phone book under that title). It may help to discover how much registered fair rents are for similar premises in the same area. You can do this by inspecting the Rent Officer's register. There is no charge for this.

The Rent Officer generally calls at the premises to take down various details of the property, room measurements, and so on, and may then invite both landlord and tenant to meet at the rent office for a consultation. He will decide on a fair rent for the property and notify both parties. If either landlord or tenant objects to the Rent Officer's decision, there is in most cases a right of objection to a Rent Assessment Committee who will then determine the amount. When you are informed of the Rent Officer's decision you will also be told how you can object where you have the right to do so.

What is the effect of a registration of a fair rent?

The advantage to the tenant is obvious: he may enjoy his tenancy without fear of a sudden increase in his rent as the landlord cannot charge more than the fair rent (other than in certain limited circumstances). If the Rent Officer fixes a fair rent lower than before the landlord must reduce the rent. However, bear in mind that the fair rent may be fixed at an amount higher than the one currently paid, so the landlord could put the rent up. This is why it is advisable for you to inspect the register of fair rents first. If the rent is registered as more than is presently paid, the landlord cannot put it up straight away to the full registered rent. It is subject to certain phasing: for example, the maximum increase during the first year is half of the total increase.

Complaints that the landlord wants the tenant out

If you have what is known as a 'periodic tenancy' – one that is by week, month, or some other period with no end date fixed – your landlord must serve a valid notice to quit in order to get you to move. The notice must:

■ be in writing
■ be given **at least** four weeks before the date specified for you to leave
■ inform you of your rights in this situation

If you want to remain as the tenant check first that a proper notice to quit has been served. If it does not conform to the points mentioned you can ignore it. If for example the notice has only given you two weeks to leave you cannot be lawfully evicted in staying past the two week period. Such an eviction would be a criminal offence. If this looks like happening, make a formal complaint at the Town Clerk's Office.

Secondly, even if a proper notice to quit has been served but you want to remain and have the stomach for a bit of a battle, your landlord cannot evict you without obtaining a Court order, and he cannot apply for this until the notice to quit has run out. It does not necessarily follow, of course, that the landlord will succeed in getting a Court order to gain possession of the property.

The County Court[2] may make such an order for possession where:

■ the tenant is offered suitable alternative accommodation. Whether it is suitable will depend on a number of factors: its size, rent, situation and so on
■ the tenant is behind with his rent. He can pay it any time before the Court hearing
■ the tenant is in breach of the tenancy agreement
■ the tenant has damaged the property
■ the property has been used for illegal or immoral purposes
■ the tenant has caused a nuisance to neighbours
■ a tenant has sub-let without the landlord's authority
■ the landlord requires the accommodation for himself or his family to live in permanently, perhaps on returning home from abroad

Note that the landlord cannot simply allege that one of these conditions applies – he must prove it.

If you intend to contest any of these issues in Court, you should obtain specialist advice from the Citizens Advice Bureau or a solicitor. You may even be able to qualify for advice and representation by a solicitor under the Legal Aid and Advice Schemes (see pages 163 and 164). In this way the fees you would have to pay would either be reduced or waived.

Complaints that the landlord is not maintaining or repairing the property as he should

This is one of the most common complaints that tenants have against their landlords. The law on the subject is reasonably clear. If the tenancy is for less than seven years the landlord **must** maintain and repair the structure of the property, and also all facilities such as plumbing and heating systems, gas and electrical fittings, drainage and guttering, and so on. These obligations on the landlord are only **minimum ones** imposed by law. Under the initial tenancy agreement the landlord may have taken on more than the minimum responsibilities.

If you want the landlord to make certain repairs to the property:

- inform him of what you want put right
- give him reasonable access to the property so that the work can be carried out
- allow him a reasonable period of time do the job (this will of course vary according to the nature of the work)
- if the landlord does not do the job within a reasonable time or simply refuses to honour his legal obligations to begin with, write him a formal letter setting out the work you want doing, informing him that he is in breach of his legal duties and that unless he undertakes to do the work within seven days you will commence legal proceedings against him. Do not refuse to pay your rent until he carries out the work as this would place you in breach of your part of the agreement
- before starting any legal action seek proper legal advice
- in certain circumstances your local authority may be able to compel the landlord to do the work

Complaints by the tenant that the landlord is harassing him

The law imposes on the landlord an obligation to allow the tenant to 'quietly enjoy' living in the property. This basically means the landlord must leave the tenant alone and not pester him at all times of the day and night, although he can arrange to inspect the property at reasonable hours.

Don't consider legal action unless all else has failed.

If you feel that your landlord is in breach of these obligations:

- ask him to stop, telling him politely but firmly that you object to whatever it is he has been doing
- if he continues, write him a formal letter requesting him to stop and warning him that you are prepared to take further action if he does not
- if he persists in his actions, report him to the local authority harassment officer who in some cases can, and will, prosecute
- you can also apply to the County Court[2] for an **injunction** – a Court order which prohibits a particular course of action. If the landlord continues after this he may be guilty of contempt of Court. An injunction ought to be considered only where reporting the landlord to the local authority has not been satisfactory or where you also want to claim compensation from him. Take legal advice first

COMPLAINTS BY LANDLORDS ABOUT TENANTS

Almost all the complaints landlords have against their tenants amount in law to one and the same – **breach of the tenancy agreement**. This may take the form of non-payment of rent, causing damage to the property, using the property for illegal or immoral purposes, and so on. If the tenant is genuinely in breach of his tenancy agreement, your ultimate step is to serve on him a proper notice to quit (see page 125), but before doing so send him a preliminary letter asking him to stop whatever course of action you are complaining about, and warning that if he does not, a notice to quit will be served. In most cases it is in the interests of both parties to resolve their differences out of Court in a civilised way.

If the tenant has not left the property after the four weeks' notice has expired, you have the right to apply to the County Court[2] for an order granting you possession of the property. You will have to prove the alleged breach in order to persuade the Court to give you possession. If the tenant looks like contesting the matter in Court, seek proper legal advice.

One very important **don't** for landlords is to harass a tenant – such a step may be regarded as a criminal offence, resulting in a prosecution by the local authority.

Complaints about squatters[3]

The Criminal Law Act 1977 contains rules which help home-owners to recover possession if they find that squatters have moved in. Ask the squatters to leave and if they fail to do so call the police who can arrest them on the spot.

Notes: Scotland and Northern Ireland

1 The Northern Irish counterpart of the Housing Aid and Advice Centre is the Northern Ireland Housing Executive Advice Centre. The Belfast Law Centre and the Citizens Advice Bureau may also be able to help.

2 The Sheriff Court is the Scottish equivalent of the County Court.

3 In Scotland you should raise an action of ejection in the Sheriff Court. This is a summary procedure and can be quite speedy.

In Northern Ireland your best bet is to sue for trespass. If the property is council property, get advice from the local Housing Advice Centre, if private, from the Citizens Advice Bureau or a solicitor.

Complaints about employment

It is almost impossible these days to switch on the radio or television or pick up a newspaper without coming across stories of industrial disputes, pay claims, strikes, picketing and union negotiations. This section deals with the mechanics behind the stories.

COMPLAINTS BY EMPLOYEES ABOUT EMPLOYERS

Complaints by employees against their employers tend to fall into two identifiable categories:

■ An employee has some personal complaint or a grievance of a very general nature, one that does not at the initial stages seem to have any legal

for forty years loyal service to the firm...

consequences. For example, he may dislike the way the business or company is being run, or think that the boss is being rude, is disgruntled about the lack of promotion prospects, or considers he is underpaid.

■ An employee feels his legal rights have been infringed: for example, he has been unfairly dismissed, or received less redundancy money than he considers he is entitled to.

In short, complaints and disputes generally occur because of the way an employee or employees have been treated either over some disciplinary matter or because they have a sense of grievance over some personal issue of importance to them. It is possible in a book of this kind to give only a very general presentation of the main organisations an employee may turn to for help with his complaint. To give a more comprehensive coverage would be unfeasible given the diversity and complexity of the situations which may arise and the volume of law on the subject.

General information

The Employment Protection (Consolidation) Act 1978[1] imposes upon employers a legal obligation to provide an employee with a written statement about the main terms of his contract of employment within 13 weeks of the employee starting work. The statement must:

■ specify any disciplinary rules which are to apply to the employee, or mention an accessible document which states the rules
■ specify the person, either by position or name, to whom the employee can refer if he is dissatisfied with any disciplinary decision relating to him, and the name of the person to whom he can air a grievance

If you want to know whether or not you have a valid complaint against your employer in an issue involving the way you have been treated over some disciplinary matter, your starting point for information is the written statement containing details of the disciplinary rules.

Code of Practice

As a supplement to this written statement, and indeed to provide a foundation on which disciplinary procedures in general are to be built, The Advisory Conciliation and Arbitration Service[2] (ACAS – more about them later in the chapter) have issued a Code of Practice which all the employers should adhere to (copies are available free from ACAS). Failure by an employer to observe a provision of the Code of Practice is not in itself a breach of any legal obligation, but the fact that he is not observing the rules of the game is admissible in evidence at an industrial tribunal, and may be used as an indication that he has acted unreasonably. According to the Code, disciplinary procedures should:

- be in writing
- specify to whom they apply
- provide for any matter to be dealt with quickly
- indicate the disciplinary actions which may be taken
- specify the various levels of management which have authority to take forms of disciplinary action, ensuring that immediate superiors do not normally have the power to dismiss without reference to senior management
- provide for individuals to be informed of the complaints against them and to be given an opportunity to state their side of the matter before decisions are reached
- give individuals the right to be accompanied by a trade union representative or by a fellow employee of their choice
- ensure that, except for gross misconduct, no employee is dismissed for a first breach of discipline
- ensure that disciplinary action is not taken until the case has been carefully investigated
- ensure that an individual is given an explanation of any penalty imposed
- provide a right of appeal and specify the procedure to be followed

Complaints that an employee's legal rights have been infringed

Suppose you consider that you have been unfairly dismissed, or discriminated against, on the grounds of your sex or race, or that your legal rights have been infringed in some other manner. How might you handle such a situation and where might you get help?

If your complaint is based on the way you have been treated over some disciplinary matter, check your employer's disciplinary rules and make sure that they conform to the Code of Practice.

If you feel the need to take the matter further, find out the procedure for registering a formal grievance. In many unionised firms the unions have negotiated a formal grievance procedure with the employers. If there is one use it – the written particulars will have details of it. If there is no formal grievance procedure the written particulars should at least specify the name of the person to whom you should complain initially.

If you are a member of a union speak to your local representative. Many unions are in a position to be able to give legal advice and even to conduct your case for you. If nothing else they may advise you that your case is poor and not worth pursuing.

As a final resort you can in most cases take the matter before an industrial tribunal (see page 157). These are examples of complaints against employers that employees have taken before an industrial tribunal:

- unfair dismissal
- unequal pay

- sex discrimination
- racial discrimination
- infringement of maternity rights including maternity pay
- prohibition of trade union membership and activities
- no time off before imminent redundancy to look for work or arrange for training
- no time off for public duties
- lack of written statement of reasons for dismissal
- unitemised pay statements
- certain matters concerning redundancy

Complaints involving personal grievances

You may have some personal grievance against your employer which has no legal implication. For example, perhaps you have been passed over the the tenth time for promotion, or you seem to be given all the rotten jobs to do, or you aren't satisfied with the facilities provided by your employer. Where do you go to deal with complaints of that type? The steps to take are very similar to those when your legal rights have been infringed except that you have no recourse to a tribunal hearing.

Follow the formal grievance procedure negotiated by your union, or complain to the person specified in your written particulars.

Talk to your union. They will have more bargaining strength than you on your own and will often help.

If the issue is particularly serious you might consider industrial action. It should be stressed that such action should be embarked on only after all other more peaceful attempts at resolution have been made. Remember that in any fight, both sides get hurt, regardless of the ultimate result.

COMPLAINTS BY EMPLOYERS ABOUT EMPLOYEES

The sort of complaints that employers have against their employees tend to fall into one of two categories:

A complaint about some general personal matter

This might be an objection to the length of an employee's hair, lack of tie, or his rudeness to customers. Employees are under a legal obligation to adhere to all 'reasonable' requests and instructions, so failure to do so may give rise to disciplinary action. A wise employer should attempt to make his special demands known from the start, perhaps by itemising them in the written particulars supplied to every new employee.

A complaint that the employee is in breach of some disciplinary matter
Employers facing disciplinary problems can obtain useful guidance on how to behave from the Code of Practice on disciplinary matters produced by ACAS.

Establish all the relevant facts as soon as possible. Talk to all parties concerned, including any witnesses, to get the best picture you can. In particularly serious cases you might even consider a short period of suspension while you make your investigations.

Make sure the employee is given an opportunity to present his side of the story, accompanied if he wants. **Do not** impose any form of penalty until after this step has been taken.

If you establish that some disciplinary action is required, adopt the following procedure where possible: in matters of a minor nature give the employee a formal oral warning. If you regard the matter as more serious issue a written warning specifying what the employee has done wrong and informing him of the consequences if he does it again.

If the employee persists with his misbehaviour, send him a final written warning telling him that any further similar offence will result in dismissal, suspension or some other penalty.

Finally if the employee takes no notice you can bring to bear whatever penalty you have threatened.

By following these guidelines you will be able to prove that you acted reasonably and in line with the Code of Practice should the employee take up the matter with his union or, in the case of dismissal, at an industrial tribunal. Instant (summary) dismissal is inadvisable unless the disciplinary breach was so blatant and serious that your actions were considered reasonable in the circumstances. Even in such cases an employee must be offered an opportunity to give his side of the story.

If the employee in question is a trade union official, it is advisable to take no action other than give an oral warning until the matter has been discussed with a senior trade union representative.

THE ADVISORY, CONCILIATION AND ARBITRATION SERVICE (ACAS)

Regardless of whether you are an employer or an employee and regardless of the kind of employment complaint you have, ACAS is likely to be the organisation most helpful to you.

Don't be afraid to seek expert advice when you feel you can't handle the situation yourself.

What is ACAS?

The Advisory, Conciliation and Arbitration Service[2] is an independent statutory body whose function is to give free and impartial help and information to everyone concerned with employment.

- **Advisory** It operates an advisory and general information service about employment matters for anyone who requires it. For example, the Yorkshire and Humberside Branch receives 500–600 requests for advice and information a week, many of them by telephone.
- **Conciliation** In this context 'conciliate' means that a specially trained officer will act as a mediator between an employer and an employee who are in conflict. It works in two ways: **Informal and voluntary conciliation** Either side at any stage in their conflict can ask for the assistance of a conciliation officer. For example an employee who is considering taking his case to an industrial tribunal may ask ACAS for help as a peacemaker before taking this more drastic step. At such a request a conciliation officer will visit both sides, perhaps more than once, to see if he can bring about a peaceful resolution of the dispute. This type of conciliation will in no way prejudice an employee's right to take further action in a tribunal.
  Formal Conciliation Once a party has completed an industrial tribunal application form (IT 1) and sent it off, ACAS will automatically receive a copy of the form. It is then under a statutory duty to send along a conciliation officer to see if a peaceful settlement may be reached.
- **Arbitration** The kind of disputes in which ACAS is usually asked to provide an arbitration service is between unions and management. When a deadlock in a particular dispute is reached the parties can jointly agree that ACAS, as an arbitration board, should examine all the details of the dispute and make an award. Although these awards are not legally binding, because arbitration itself is usually chosen by both parties any award is usually accepted.

Notes: Scotland and Northern Ireland

1 In Northern Ireland the Industrial Relations (Northern Ireland) Order 1976 (amended in 1982) is largely the same as the Employment Protection (Consolidation) Act 1978.

2 ACAS does not operate in Northern Ireland. The corresponding body is the Labour Relations Agency in Belfast (there is a Londonderry branch – see Address section).

Complaints about discrimination

Despite society's attempts in recent times to provide equality of opportunity for all, it is still the case that some people are treated more equally than others. This section sets out to explain how you can complain if you feel you have been discriminated against either on racial grounds or because of your sex, and what you might gain by making a complaint.

COMPLAINTS ABOUT RACIAL DISCRIMINATION

The Race Relations Act 1976[1] makes it unlawful to discriminate against another person on racial grounds: their colour, race, nationality or ethnic origins. The Act does not make such discrimination a criminal offence, but recognises that it amounts to a serious infringement of a person's legal rights, and as such gives that person the right to take legal action either at an industrial tribunal (for employment matters) or a designated County Court[2] (for other matters). In this way a suitable remedy or redress may be obtained.

The Commission for Racial Equality is the official body set up by the Race Relations Act 1976 to advise and assist those with complaints involving discrimination. The CRE has two distinct functions, both of which are useful to would-be complainants.

- It acts as a law enforcement agency by advising you and often by giving positive representation in bringing a complaint to Court.
- It also acts as an agency to promote awareness of minority needs. In this sense it acts almost as a pressure group. If you have a general complaint about the way a minority group has been unfairly treated the Commission is interested to hear about it and may take up the matter.

How will the Commission help?

- It will be able to give general advice on your case.
- It will provide you with a special questionnaire to send to the person you are complaining about. The Race Relations Act gives you the right to send this out in order to find out at an early stage the other side of the case and so decide whether or not to pursue your complaint in Court.

135

- If you decide to go ahead the Commission will advise you on the procedures and presentation of your case.
- In some circumstances it will represent you and pay your costs. You should complete one of the Commission's special green forms which will enable it to consider what help it can give you. If you need help in completing the form contact your nearest Community Relations Council, Law Centre or Citizens Advice Bureau, or ask the Commission itself. In addition to the London Office there are offices in Birmingham, Leeds, Leicester and Manchester (the Manchester office covers Scotland).

Racial discrimination in employment

If your complaint is about racial discrimination in any aspect of employment, whether in the selection of employees, terms of the job, training, promotional facilities or trade union matters, these are the steps to take.

Write to the person or organisation you are alleging discrimination against, enclosing the special questionnaire mentioned above (available from the Commission, or any employment office or job centre). At its simplest the form asks the person accused of discrimination to give his side of the story. There is no compulsion on him to reply but failure to do so or answering evasively may be taken into account by an industrial tribunal should the matter get that far.

If you get no reply, or if you are not satisfied with the response and still wish to pursue the complaint, write to ACAS asking them to attempt to conciliate before you approach an industrial tribunal. A conciliation officer will attempt to settle the matter peacefully. If conciliation by ACAS proves unsuccessful make a formal complaint to an industrial tribunal.

If the tribunal upholds your complaint it may award any of the following:

- a declaration of the legal rights involved
- compensation for any loss you have suffered, including compensation for injury to feelings through the discrimination
- recommendations to the person or body complained against on the steps they should take to put matters to rights, for example offering you a job or a chance for promotion

If you are going to complain to an industrial tribunal it is vitally important that you do so within three months of the alleged discrimination taking place. If you apply after this period you may lose your right to a tribunal hearing. The application form for a tribunal hearing is known as an IT 1 and is available from the Commission, any employment office or job centre. ACAS will automatically receive a copy when you have completed it and sent it off. They must then attempt to settle the matter by conciliation, and a tribunal hearing will only take place after this has failed, perhaps for the second time if you asked for their assistance before. For more details of how to take a case to an industrial tribunal see page 157.

Racial discrimination in education

If you believe that there has been racial discrimination against you or your child by a school, college or university, the way in which you complain depends on whether your establishment is in the private or public sector of education.

- **The private sector**
  It is always worth trying to settle the matter before a formal hearing is needed, but if that fails you may bring a direct legal action against the party complained of in the appropriate County Court.[2]
- **The public sector**
  Legal action may still be brought against the authority in the County Court,[2] but only after you have referred the complaint to the Department of Education and Science,[3] who must be allowed up to two months to investigate before you bring proceedings. You should send your complaint to the Permanent Under-Secretary of State for Education at the Department of Education and Science.

Racial discrimination in housing, goods, facilities and services

If you consider that you have been discriminated against because of the colour of your skin, you can bring direct legal proceedings in the County Court[2] for breach of the Race Relations Act 1976.[1]

Racial discrimination in advertising

Only the Commission for Racial Equality can bring proceedings involving advertisements which are racially discriminatory, but you can report instances to the Commission, sending a copy of the advertisement where possible.

The Commission may investigate the matter, and if it decides that the advertisement is unlawful it can issue a 'non-discrimination notice' requiring its publication to cease.

It may take legal action either at an industrial tribunal if the case involves employment matters, or in Court for other forms of alleged discriminatory action. The purpose of this would be to establish a decision on whether an unlawful act had taken place, and if necessary to obtain an injunction – a Court order prohibiting the person responsible for the discrimination from continuing or repeating the action. Other remedies available if your complaint of racial discrimination is upheld by the Court might be a declaration on the legal rights involved, or compensation for any loss suffered, including an award for injured feelings.

General tips on complaining about racial discrimination

- Get help from the Commission for Racial Equality.
- Don't delay. There are very narrow time limits in which you have to complain. You have three months in which to complain to an industrial tribunal and six months to complain to a County Court,[2] although if you make an application to the Commission for assistance by completing the 'green form'[4] (details on page 163) this extends the time limit by one month.
- Depending on your means you may be entitled to legal advice and representation under the Legal Aid and Advice Schemes (see pages 163 and 164). If you qualify you may receive legal services either free of charge or at a reduced rate. The Commission may also support you financially.

COMPLAINTS ABOUT SEX DISCRIMINATION

The Sex Discrimination Act 1975 makes it unlawful for a member of one sex to be treated less favourably than a member of the other simply because of their sex. Although the Act talks in terms of discrimination against women, it applies equally to protect men. The Act does not make sex discrimination a criminal offence but it does give individuals discriminated against the right to bring a civil action either in an industrial tribunal where an employment matter is involved, or the County Court[2] where some other discriminatory issue is alleged to have taken place. A statutory body was set up specially to provide assistance in cases of sex discrimination – the Equal Opportunities Commission (the EOC).

How will the Equal Opportunities Commission help?

- It investigates and conducts research into the entire area of sex discrimination and makes recommendations to the Government about the operation of existing laws.
- It offers free general advice on matters concerning sex discrimination.
- If you have a specific complaint it will look at all the details, and advise you what to do next.
- Sometimes it can give 'formal assistance'. This may amount to acting as a peacemaker between you and the other party to try to reach a settlement. Some or all of the cost of your case may even be paid for. It is by no means certain that formal assistance will be offered in every case, but you should apply for it anyway and see what the EOC says. A special form is available from the Commission.

Making your complaint

- **Advice** It is always a good idea to seek expert advice before taking any action at all – you are in a much stronger position if you know precisely what your legal rights are in the issue. The EOC will always help. If your case involves something in the employment field you should consult ACAS (see page 134) who will not only give general advice but will also attempt to resolve the dispute peacefully without the need for an industrial tribunal hearing.
- **Send out a questionnaire** The Sex Discrimination Act gives the complainant the right to send the other party a questionnaire asking about specific areas of the complaint. This serves three very useful functions. It shows that you mean business which may make a settlement easier, it will provide you with valuable information about the other person's side of the story which will help you decide whether to pursue the complaint, and further the replies are admissible as evidence either in Court or at an industrial tribunal.

- **Time** Once you have made a firm decision to go ahead with a formal complaint by taking legal action, don't delay. There are strict time limits within which you must make your complaint: these vary depending on the circumstances.

Type of sex discrimination

- **Equal pay** The Equal Pay Act 1970 states that men and women doing the same or broadly similar work have the right to receive the same wages and terms of employment. If you are still in the job you can claim any time. If you have left you must make a claim to the industrial tribunal within six months of leaving. Complete form IT1, available from the EOC, job centres or any employment office.
- **Jobs and Training** (includes promotion) Claims to the industrial tribunal must be made within three months of the discrimination. Complete form IT1.
- **Education in state institutions** (not universities) Claim in the County Court[2] within eight months but first approach the Education Minister in writing who has two months to look into your complaint.
- **Private education and universities** Claim to the County Court[2] within six months.
- **Housing, goods, facilities and services** Claim to the County Court[2] within six months.

Where a Court or industrial tribunal decides in your favour it may award any of the following remedies:

- **Compensation** for any loss you have suffered because of the discrimination, including a sum for injury to your feelings.
- **A declaration** on the rights and wrongs of the case.
- **An injunction** (only in Court). This amounts to an order to a particular body or person to cease specified acts.
- **Recommendations** (in an industrial tribunal). This may be directions to the employer on how to put matters to rights, for example by offering you promotional opportunities.

Sex discrimination in advertising

As with racially discriminatory advertisements you cannot take legal action yourself over one you judge to be sexually discriminatory but you should report the advertisement to the Equal Opportunities Commission. They can issue a 'non-discrimination notice' requiring publication of the advertisement to stop, or they can apply to the court to determine whether the advertisement is in breach of the law, and if so to seek an injunction prohibiting its further publication.

Notes: Scotland and Northern Ireland

1 In practice, The Race Relations Act 1976 applies in Northern Ireland only to a very limited extent.

2 Throughout the chapter the Sheriff Court in Scotland may be taken to serve the same functions as the County Court in England and Wales.

3 In Scotland, refer a complaint about racial discrimination in education in the public sector to the Secretary of the Scottish Education Department.

4 The 'green form' is pink in Scotland.

Complaints about advertising

There are two controlling influences on advertising, both of which provide the public with a possible channel through which to register a complaint.

- **The law**

  There are numerous Acts of Parliament which seek to control advertising in some way. The most comprehensive of these is the Trade Descriptions Act 1968 (see later). The Sex Discrimination Act 1975 and the Race Relations Act 1976 also both have a role to play in statutory advertising control. See pages 135 and 138.

- **Self-regulatory controls**

  In addition to the legal constraints on advertising there exists a code to which advertisers must adhere – the British Code of Advertising Practice. The Advertising Standards Authority (ASA), a voluntary organisation financed by the advertising industry and backed by the Office of Fair Trading, has the responsibility for supervising general standards and investigating complaints that an advertiser may be in breach of the Code. The ASA can deal with print, poster and cinema advertising but not television or radio commercials: these are handled by the Independent Broadcasting Authority (more details on page 145).

HOW THE LAW CAN HELP

Criminal law

The Trade Descriptions Act 1968 makes it a criminal offence to give false or misleading information about goods for sale and their prices. This would be the case even if the wrong information were given innocently. The Act covers the provision of services as well as goods.

If you believe such an offence has been committed report it to the Trading Standards Department[1] – their address will be in the phone book under the local authority section. They will investigate your complaint and depending on all the circumstances may bring a prosecution against those responsible for the advertisement. If a conviction is brought the offender is usually fined although he may sometimes receive a prison sentence. In addition to passing sentence, under the Powers of Criminal Courts Act 1973[2] the Court is able to award the victim or victims compensation. Remember too that proceedings and investigations into a matter involving a possible breach of the Trade Descriptions Act 1968 are carried out at the expense of the local authority.

There is one qualifying factor about the Trade Descriptions Act: it applies only to advertisements made by traders and does not cover, for instance, goods sold through the private sales column of a newspaper. Criminal law cannot usually help here – you must look to civil law for a suitable remedy.

Civil law

The Sale of Goods Act 1979 states that it is implicit in every contract when goods are sold (including private ones) that they will correspond to the description given. If they do not the seller is in breach of contract and the buyer is entitled to his money back.

Before commencing any legal action you should always give the person about whom you are complaining the opportunity of putting things right. Legal action should only be used as a last resort when all other means have failed.

COMPLAINTS ABOUT NEWSPAPER, MAGAZINE, CINEMA AND POSTER ADVERTISEMENTS

The Advertising Standards Authority (ASA)

The first page of the British Code of Advertising Practice declares that 'All advertisements should be legal, decent, honest and truthful'. Very simply the job of the ASA is to see that these ideals are put into practice, using the Code as a set of rules. The Code covers not only these general standards but specific problems arising from advertising certain products including cigarettes and alcohol. The ASA is therefore keen for people to tell them about advertisements in magazines, newspapers, on posters, or at the cinema (not on television and radio) which they regard as offensive or misleading in some way.

How to complain

Write to the Advertising Standards Authority, giving as much detail about your objections to the advertisements as you can – what it is about, where it is and so on. Where possible send a copy of the advertisement.

A decision will be made on whether or not the complaint is to be pursued, and if so in what way. If the complaint contains allegations of a possible breach of the Code of Practice it will certainly be investigated.

If the ASA decides that there is a case to answer it sends a letter to the advertiser involved, setting out the complaint and inviting comments. If the case appears to be very serious, the advertiser may be asked to stop advertising until the investigation has been completed and a decision reached.

The advertiser must now reply in writing to the complaint. He must attempt

143

to substantiate the claim made in his advertisement, and must be seen to be doing so without delay.

The ASA then evaluates all the evidence. It may also require further information, perhaps from an expert where technical matters are involved. At the end of the investigation a draft recommendation is submitted to the ASA Council, with copies sent to complainant and advertiser. The Council makes the final decision.

What is the effect of a complaint?

If it is decided that the advertiser is in breach of the Code of Practice he is asked to undertake not to repeat it and either to amend or withdraw the offending advertisement. If he refuses to give such an undertaking the ASA informs a number of media organisations that are members of the Code of Advertising Practice Committee that in its judgement the advertisement or claim concerned contravenes the Code. All members have given an undertaking that advertising space will not be available to any advertisement which contains material in breach of the Code.

The outcome of the complaint, the names of advertisers and their advertisements are published in the case reports, available free on request from the ASA.

The ASA has no power to order an advertiser to pay you any compensation even if you have suffered loss as a result of a false or misleading advertisement. By complaining you are seeing that high advertising standards are maintained

for the benefit of all consumers. If you are after some personal compensatory redress you must look to the law for a remedy (see earlier in the chapter). Making a complaint to the ASA is not necessarily in place of taking legal action but is an additional method of imposing pressure on the advertiser and may provide you with some useful evidence.

COMPLAINTS ABOUT RADIO AND TELEVISION ADVERTISEMENTS

The report of the Independent Broadcasting Authority (IBA) annually shows that though several thousand television and radio advertisements are broadcast only a few hundred letters of complaint are received and only a handful upheld. The reason for so few justified complaints is a very comprehensive and rigid monitoring system. All scripts for television advertisements (other than local advertisements) must be cleared by the Independent Television Companies' Association (ITCA) and the IBA. Before they are accepted for broadcasting they are checked for suitability, claims must be substantiated, and the entire package must be examined in light of the IBA Code of Advertising Standards and Practice. Amendments to the script may be suggested before final clearance is given. A similar system operates for radio commercials: the clearance method is operated jointly by ITCA and the Association of Independent Radio Contractors (AIRC).

How to complain
If you do have cause to complain, however, don't be put off by the statistics – write to the Independent Broadcasting Authority who will ensure that your complaint is looked into. Give them all the details about the advertisement: when you saw it, where it was broadcast, and what you think is wrong with it. Complaints upheld recently include a radio commercial for a comedy film found to have an unacceptable degree of sexual innuendo; and a television commercial shown just before Christmas, showing a well-known comedian stealing goods from a stage display, found to condone shoplifting.

Notes: Scotland and Northern Ireland

1 In Scotland, instead of the Trading Standards Department, the Procurator Fiscal will investigate your complaint and perhaps bring a prosecution against those responsible for the advertisements.

   Complaints about incorrect or offensive advertising in Northern Ireland can go either to the Trading Standards Branch of the Department of Economic Development for Northern Ireland, or directly to the Office of Fair Trading.

2 In Scotland and Northern Ireland victims may receive compensation under the Criminal Justice Act 1980, a separate version applying in each country.

145

Complaints about the media

COMPLAINTS ABOUT THE PRESS

You don't like what a newspaper or magazine has written about you: perhaps you have been totally misquoted in something you said. Or perhaps a reporter and photographer have hounded you to get an interview out of you. If you have such a complaint or indeed any similar grievance against the press, there is a series of actions you can take.

- complain to the editor of the newspaper of magazine
- refer the matter to the Press Council
- take legal action where this is appropriate and possible

Complaining to the editor

If you have a grievance a letter of complaint to the editor should be your first course of action. If one of his staff has behaved improperly towards you he will want to know about it and will certainly do something to put matters to rights. If you feel a story published about you or some matter you are connected with gives a false and unfair impression, you might ask and eventually insist that the editor publish a prompt apology.

However, a word of warning here: if you think that the newspaper has printed something about you which is libellous (see page 149) and that you might sue, don't write to the newspaper without seeking legal advice first. If you did you might say something which could prejudice your chances of suing successfully later on. If dealing with the editor proves unsatisfactory complain to the Press Council within two months.

The Press Council

The Press Council is the 'watchdog' of the British press. Its main work is dealing with complaints made by the public against newspapers and magazines. The Council consists of an independent lay chairman, and 18 representatives each of the press and the public.

Complaints it can and cannot deal with

It can look into any complaints about published material apart from advertising matter (for advertising see page 142). It can examine complaints about the way the press operates to get material, or indeed any issues where the general standards of the press are called into question since one of its main aims is

to maintain the character of the British press in accordance with the highest professional and commercial standards.

It cannot investigate individual complaints where financial compensation is sought; and it can't look into complaints which might result in a Court case. The Press Council would probably ask you to sign a form waiving all your legal rights against the publication concerned before looking into your complaint.

How to make a complaint to the Press Council

Although in many cases an attempt to resolve the complaint through correspondence with the editor of the journal or newspaper concerned will have been made, there is no absolute necessity to do this and a complainant may choose to refer the complaint to the Press Council from the outset.

Write to the Director of the Press Council enclosing:

- a statement of your complaint, saying what you think was improper or wrong on the part of the newspaper, periodical or journal
- copies of any letters to or from the editor or those acting for him

- the page of the newspaper or periodical containing the matter at the centre of your complaint (if appropriate)
- a signed and dated statement by any witnesses (if your complaint involves any allegation that you were grossly misquoted in an interview, such a statement may be of use)

It is important that you make your complaint within two months of the issue taking place.

What will the Press Council do?

- **It will conciliate** The Council has a conciliation procedure for mediating between you and the editor of the publication but it is only used if both parties give consent, and does not prejudice the position of either party if the case goes further.
- **It will investigate** If conciliation is not tried or fails to resolve the complaint, the assistant director and his staff investigate on behalf of the Council. They may write to you seeking further information or clarification. If you show that there may have been a breach of recognised standards of press conduct, the Press Council puts the complaint and the collected evidence to the editor concerned for him to answer. He is also asked to put the matter to any journalists involved.

    All the relevant information will then be considered by the Complaints Committee who may do one of three things:

    - say there is no case to answer and halt the investigation
    - call for further evidence
    - recommend a finding to the Council

Although the complaints committee usually arrives at its decision purely on the basis of written evidence, the editors and journalists involved have the right to appear before the committee to explain their side of the case. Where this right of appearance is exercised, you too are given the opportunity to present oral evidence. The whole thing may therefore become an informal oral hearing.

After the complaints committee has considered a complaint, its recommendations are passed by the Council for a final adjudication. The Council's decision is usually published in the press. This operates as a big stick to the offending newspaper or journal as clearly it threatens its public credibility.

Take legal action

If you feel that something a newspaper or other publication has published about you is untrue and has caused damage to your reputation, you might consider taking legal action for libel. But beware that such an action is not something you should attempt on your own and can be expensive because you have to sue in the High Court. See a solicitor for advice about your chances of success.

COMPLAINTS ABOUT RADIO AND TELEVISION

If you have a complaint about something which has been broadcast on television or radio, there are three main avenues for pursuing your complaint.

- the radio or television company responsible for the broadcast
- the Broadcasting Complaints Commission
- the Courts

The Radio/Television Company responsible

If you want to complain about the content or quality of a particular programme, or programmes in general, it is the individual broadcasting companies them-selves to whom you should complain. For example, if you feel that the BBC are showing too much sex on television, give them a phone call and tell them. On the other hand if you are upset that an independent company is not showing enough sex, ring and point this out. All the broadcasting companies will receive and record your complaints and comments. Some even have special telephone lines to deal with them. Don't be afraid to air your views in this way – after all it is only right that the broadcasters should be kept informed of the needs and feelings of their public.

The Broadcasting Complaints Commission

The Broadcasting Complaints Commission was set up in June 1981. Its job is to consider and adjudicate complaints made to it about radio or television programmes, advertisements and teletext transmissions broadcast either by the BBC or the IBA.

What complaints can the Commission deal with?
The scope of the Commission is in reality extremely limited. It can investigate a complaint only if it falls into one of the following categories:

- **Unjust or unfair treatment** Where you have participated in a programme, or have had some direct interest in the programme and feel you have been treated unfairly, you could complain to the Commission
- **'Unwarranted infringement of privacy'** This seems to apply not only to the content of a programme but also to the way the material for a programme was obtained. If you have a complaint of this nature, it is within the power of the Commission to investigate it.

What complaints the Commission cannot deal with

- Complaints about the general quality and content of programmes – these should be made directly to the broadcasting companies responsible, as dealt with on page 149.
- Complaints which are or might be the subject of Court proceedings.

How to complain

If you feel that your complaint is one that the Commission has power to deal with, put your complaint in writing, giving as many details as possible and send it to the Broadcasting Complaints Commission. The Commission will check first to see that the matter is within its power to investigate and if so a copy of the complaint will be passed to the broadcasting body responsible, inviting its comments. Depending on the response of the broadcasters, it may prove necessary to make further enquiries, so an informal hearing will be held to enable the Commission to get all the relevant details. Having done so it will consider all the facts and issue a written adjudication to all the parties involved.

It is important to note that even if your complaint is upheld the Commission can offer you very little by way of a positive remedy, and it certainly has no power to award any compensation. All it can do is direct the broadcasting body concerned to publish the adjudication in the national press.

In the Courts

If you feel that a statement about you in a radio or television programme is both untrue and damaging to your reputation, you might well be able to seek an appropriate remedy in the Courts, such as compensation for libel. However, a word of warning; libel actions can be expensive and should not even be contemplated without first seeing a solicitor experienced in such cases.

Taking legal action

THE COUNTY COURT[1]

Most of the sections in the book so far have been devoted to complaints against specific bodies or organisations and how best to use any complaints procedures that may exist. We have explained how to enlist the assistance of other interested parties, watchdogs or pressure groups to resolve your complaint in the most effective way with the least possible aggravation.

There are some cases, however, where you should recognise that if your legal rights have been infringed, the only way to enforce them is to take legal action. This part of the book sets out to summarise the basic steps for taking legal action yourself in the County Court[1] where most civil cases are heard. The procedures are very similar for a major civil case brought in the High Court but things there are rather more formal and shouldn't be contemplated without expert professional guidance throughout. Note that the emphasis in this section is on suing where you have a 'small claim' in England and Wales. See the end of the chapter on page 161 for the different systems in Scotland and Northern Ireland.

Should I sue?
Here are a few guidelines to help you decide:

- **Have you tried all other possibilities?** You should only sue as a last resort when all else has failed. If there is still some channel left, try it providing that doing so will not prejudice your chances of success.
- **Will you get your money if you win?** If you are considering suing someone for compensation, a major consideration before commencing legal action, no matter how clear-cut your case seems to be, is – have they got the money to pay if I do win?
- **How easy is it?** Where your claim is relatively small – that is £500 or less – Arbitration Proceedings will be used. This makes suing in the County Court far more informal and simple than you might have thought, and the amount of money you stand to lose is generally extremely limited. When the matter is dealt with by Arbitration the case is usually decided by a registrar, often in his private rooms (in chambers).
- **How much will it cost?** This is without doubt the biggest worry for most people. Yet in the majority of small claims the costs are much less than you

might suppose. One of the main advantages of using Arbitration Proceedings is that even if you lose you do not have to pay the other party's costs incurred in getting the services of a lawyer. But if you bring the action 'unreasonably' you may have costs awarded against you. You will still have to pay your own lawyer for his services, but if you want to dispense with them, you can handle the case yourself – the informality of Arbitration Proceedings brings this within the capabilities of many untrained people.

If the case does not go to Arbitration but is tried in Court, the costs are likely to be higher and the risks likewise. An unsuccessful party will usually have to pay the other party's legal costs. (Incidentally, you can now insure yourself against legal costs in many fields.)

The fees that have to be paid to the County Court to issue a summons either to obtain a sum of money, or to get delivery of goods, are from about 10p for every £1 for claims up to £300 (minimum fee £5), to about £35 for claims of £550. This is called the **plaint fee**.

Whether or not the case is dealt with by Arbitration, the unsuccessful party will usually have to pay the successful party his costs (lawyer's fees excluded unless not arbitrated) such as the plaint fee, travel expenses, witnesses' expenses, time off work (though this is not usually awarded).

How to sue in the County Court

Having weighed up all the pros and cons of taking the seemingly drastic step of suing someone, you then face another problem: how to do it?

Before becoming too panic-stricken, bear in mind that there are plenty of people or organisations able to assist, for example the Citizens' Advice Bureau and some Trading Standards Departments. Don't forget too the most obvious place – the County Court offices themselves. Do not hesitate to ask the assistants there for help – they should not and will not advise you on the merits of your case but will probably be extremely helpful such as explaining any procedures, filling in forms, interpreting legal jargon for you, and so on. The booklet *Small Claims in the County Court*, issued free by the Lord Chancellor's department, is a very helpful publication – you can get it from the County Court or the Citizens Advice Bureau.

Preparing your case

The first step is for you to write out what are called **Particulars of Claim** which are the full details of your case. You are the **plaintiff**, the person complaining about the action or wrongdoing of some other person, who is known as the **defendant** – the person defending the complaint. Ultimately your Particulars of Claim will be put to the defendant to offer him the opportunity of presenting a written defence. Your written particulars and his written defence form what are known as the **pleadings**.

Particulars of claim

Preparing your Particulars of Claim is a relatively simple process. You can use a form supplied by the Court Offices for the purpose, or a plain piece of paper. You will need two copies. Put at the top the name of the Court dealing with the case; for this you as the plaintiff have a choice. The case can either be heard by the County Court for the district in which the defendant resides (the registered office for a registered company is officially where a company is located), or the district in which the cause of the legal action arose. For example a consumer suing for a refund because of faulty goods could sue in the County Court for the district where the company's registered office is or in the County Court for the district in which the contract was made.

Next list the parties to the action, that is, the full names of the plaintiff and defendant. Then write the words 'Particulars of Claim', and follow this with a detailed statement of all the facts of the case. It is a good idea to set out the facts in a series of numbered paragraphs which can later be referred to by their numbers. The Particulars should fall into four separate categories – if you include them all you will be on the right lines. Take as an example the case of a consumer suing because of faulty goods:

- **details of the purchase** – date, type of goods, model number, where bought, price, etc
- **facts of the case** – this is basically an explanation of what is wrong with the goods, what has been done up to now, who said what, etc
- **law** on which you are basing your case – in this example, the fact that a particular shop is in breach of its obligations under the Sale of Goods Act 1979 should be mentioned
- **remedies** – in the last section of your Particulars of Claim you should set out exactly what you are asking for in terms of a remedy. If you are after compensation you should state what loss you are claiming for, and how much

Taking out the summons

Go to the local County Court Offices, taking the Particulars with you, in order to issue the summons. If it is inconvenient to go in person you may post the material to them. Remember to enclose the correct number of copies of the necessary forms (see below), the plaint fee and a self-addressed envelope.

It is likely that you will want to issue a **default summons** as opposed to a fixed date summons, but you should ask at the Offices. A default summons is used when you are claiming a particular sum of money, and covers claims for abstract concepts such as inconvenience, pain or emotional upset. If the defendant makes no defence within fourteen days of receiving the summons you should write to the Court asking for judgement, which is an order to the defendant from the Court to pay the sum you are asking. This does not happen automatically – you need to apply for it. A **fixed date summons** is only used where you are claiming something other than money, such as the return of goods.

Whichever summons you are issuing, if you are suing a company you will need to know its registered office. You may have found this out already when deciding which County Court to bring the proceedings in. By law every registered company must print on its letterhead the address of its registered office but if for some reason you can't discover the address this way, try asking the company directly. In any event you can find out by visiting the Search Room at Companies' Registration Office in London (no postal enquiries; £1 fee for every search) or by writing to the Office's Cardiff address.

You are now in a position to issue the summons formally. You will have to complete a form that may look a little daunting but it is simply a series of questions about the parties and their names and addresses. All the hard work has already been done in the drafting of the Particulars of Claim, so don't give in at this stage.

The form is divided into two halves, requesting information firstly about the plaintiff and secondly about the defendant. There are twelve questions:

1 asks for you the plaintiff's name and address
2 asks whether you are suing in a representative capacity – an example of this would be if you were suing someone as an executor for a deceased person
3 asks about suing as a 'next friend' – this would be someone suing another on behalf of a minor (a person under the age of 18), for example
4 deals with whether you are suing as an **assignee** – this means you may have had the right to sue transferred to you by another person who initially had the right to sue. Let's suppose Smith still owes Cheapo Ltd £100 for goods he has received and has been using. After doing everything in its power to obtain the money short of taking legal action, Cheapo Ltd (the **assignor**) sells the right to sue Smith to someone else, perhaps a debt collector, who then takes on Cheapo's rights. He is called assignee
5 & 6 are concerned with partnership and company details, if applicable.

The section dealing with the defendant is equally straightforward as it asks virtually the same questions. In question 12, if you are suing a company, this is where you insert the address of its registered office.

The final question on the form asks what the claim is for. Keep your answer short: your details are all in the Particulars of Claim so all that you would need to put would be 'Compensation for breach of contract' if you were suing for a refund for defective goods, or 'Compensation for negligence' if it were a case about a road or other accident.

Your final job is to state on the form how much you are claiming. Remember again the detailed breakdown of this on your Particulars of Claim. You will need to put in the plaint fee (the amount the Court will charge you for their services; check with them how much this will be). Take an extra copy of the form for yourself, hand over two copies, and pay your fee. All that is left to be done is for the summons to be served on the defendant. You could send it by post or deliver it yourself, or for an extra fee of £4 you can get the Court bailiff to serve the summons for you, which is probably less troublesome.

The response to the summons
Once the summons has been served, one of four things is likely to happen.

- Having seen that you really mean business the defendant simply admits liability and pays the amount you are asking for.
- The defendant, while not admitting liability, shows his willingness to settle out of Court. He usually offers a lesser sum than that claimed by you, hoping he can tempt you to accept and not proceed any further. This may mean you have a difficult decision to make: for example, suppose you are claiming £200 but are offered £100 as a settlement: it is hard to know at what point to be tempted to settle. Only you can make this decision, but preferably with the advice of a person with some experience of these matters. Once the defendant has indicated his willingness to settle you can often negotiate a higher sum provided you don't ask for too much. Two important pieces of advice on settlement:
  1. Make sure that in any letter of negotiation about a settlement you head the letter with the expression 'without prejudice'. This means that the contents cannot be referred to if and when a trial ever takes place
  2. If you do accept a settlement, make sure that the money has actually been paid into Court before you write to the Court to let them know formally that you are abandoning your case.
- The defendant will file a defence to your allegations. They will also possibly ask for more details than those stated in your initial Particulars. Be warned – they may ask for information which they assume you are unable to give, in the hope that you will be intimidated both by such a request and indeed by the fact that they appear to be going to fight the case tooth and nail to the bitter end. Give them whatever further information you want to and are capable of giving them, and if it is not possible to provide all the information they want, tell them why. If a defence is made, stop and think, and search your conscience. Go through the whole case yet again, and only if you are sure that you are still on a firm footing should you continue.
- The defendant will ignore the summons. If this is the case and if the summons was a 'default' summons, after fourteen days you will automatically get judgement (be informed that you've won the case) without having to attend the Court. To enter judgement at this stage all you have to do is to complete a simple form and return it to the County Court.

Complaining is not a pastime, nor is it a profession. Examine your conscience and complain only when it is necessary.

Pre-trial review

This is a preliminary look at all the facts by the registrar to determine if there is any way the parties may resolve their differences before going to the ultimate stage of arbitration or trial. If no such agreement can be reached the registrar will do what he can by way of preparation to make the actual hearing itself run as smoothly as possible. For example, it is at the pre-trial review stage that the parties usually agree on the number of witnesses they will be calling (try to insist on one only to keep everything in proportion), whether or not there is to be discovery (inspection of each other's documents) and the date of the final hearing. The pre-trial review is much less formal than you might expect a Court hearing to be. If you are representing yourself, the registrar is usually sympathetic to the fact that you may not fully understand the procedures and will be as helpful as possible without being biased either way.

The hearing

Regardless of whether the case is being dealt with by arbitration or a full Court hearing the basic procedure tends to be the same. In order to succeed it is for you the plaintiff to prove your case. You must convince the judge or registrar that your claim is justified. If you are to do this, the more thoroughly you prepare your case, the more likely you are to succeed. Here are some tips:

- Obtain and be ready to present to the court all the available evidence. Make sure all your witnesses are available to give evidence personally. A written statement from a witness is not as convincing or as useful as a personal appearance.
- Obtain and bring along any relevant documents, letters, invoices, receipts and so on to back up the points you make.
- Work out in advance what you want to say to the Court and make notes. Don't leave it to chance or inspiration.
- As you know who the defendant's witnesses will be, make a list of the questions you want to ask them.
- Give some serious consideration to the arguments the other side is likely to put forward, and be ready with replies to counter them.
- Take the trouble to find out about the Court procedures before your hearing takes place. All County Courts are open to the public so you can sit in and watch the proceedings.

Arbitration hearings are conducted in private, but the basic procedure is the same and will be as follows:

1. Opening statement by the plaintiff
2. The plaintiff calls witness(es) (one may be the plaintiff himself) to give evidence
3. The defendant cross-examines the plaintiff's witness(es)
4. The plaintiff re-examines the witness(es)

5. Opening statement by the defendant
6. His witnesses are called to give evidence and to be cross- and re-examined as with the plaintiff's
7. The defendant sums up his case
8. The plaintiff sums up his case
9. The judgement is usually given

If you win, the other side should pay any damages to the Court who will forward the money to you in due course. If you lose, there may in some cases be a right of appeal. At this stage you should definitely seek professional legal advice.

TAKING YOUR CASE TO AN INDUSTRIAL TRIBUNAL

If you feel that your legal rights have been infringed over some employment matter, as discussed in the chapter on page 129, your ultimate course is to take the case before an industrial tribunal. This section of the book tells you how to do this, how to prepare your case, and what you might expect to gain.

Useful points to know

Seek advice on whether in law you have a case or not. A Tribunal hearing can be more informal than a Court hearing, but it can only operate within the scope of current employment law. A decision will not go in your favour simply because the tribunal feels sorry for you or because your employers have behaved unprofessionally. You will only get a favourable decision if you can show that you have a legal right to be treated in a particular way and that this right has been infringed.

The Department of Employment[2] has prepared many free leaflets, available from your local employment office, explaining your legal rights on almost all areas of employment law. The Citizens Advice Bureau can usually assist with preliminary advice on the strength of your case, and of any legal points you ought to know about. ACAS also operates a telephone advisory service. Its officers will not give an opinion on whether you will win or lose, but they can explain to you any legal issues or technical matters they feel you should be aware of. You could seek the help of a solicitor, but although you can get general advice under the Green Form[3] Legal Advice Scheme (details on page 163), he cannot represent you at the tribunal under the Legal Aid Scheme (also explained on page 164).

Don't delay

Once you've decided definitely to go ahead with a tribunal application, don't hesitate. There are strict time limits in which your application must be made, and you may lose your rights to a hearing if your claim is submitted too late. The limit for most matters is three months from the time of the event giving rise to your complaint. In exceptional circumstances the tribunal may extend this period.

The cost
There is no fee for your application to the industrial tribunal, or indeed for the tribunal hearing itself. It is possible, even if you lose, to claim certain allowances to cover the cost of travel to a hearing for yourself, the witnesses called and your representative, so long as the latter is not a full-time official of an employer's organisation or of a trade union, or is a barrister or solicitor. Loss of your earnings and those of the witnesses may also be paid up to a specified amount. Note that costs are not usually awarded against an applicant in an industrial tribunal. However, if the tribunal decides that a person has acted 'frivolously, vexatiously or unreasonably' in bringing the case, it has the power to award costs against him.

Getting representation
You are entitled to representation at an industrial tribunal – that is, get someone to present the case on your behalf. You can be represented by a solicitor or barrister but bear in mind that you cannot get legal aid for representation at an industrial tribunal. Alternatively, you can be represented by a trade union representative, or indeed you can invite anyone you like to represent you, whether friend, spouse and so on, or you can represent yourself. The rest of this section on industrial tribunals is to help you do it yourself.

How to apply to the industrial tribunal

You need two application forms (called IT 1s) one to keep yourself, and another to send off. You can get them from your local Department of Employment Office, Job Centre or Citizens Advice Bureau. Send the completed form to the Central Office of Industrial Tribunals.

It will be acknowledged by the office and a copy sent to your employer, who is the respondent in the case (you are the applicant). The respondent must complete a form known as 'Notice of Appearance' on which he must state whether or not he intends to contest the case, and if so on what grounds. A date for the hearing will then be fixed. Meanwhile, the Central Office for Industrial Tribunals will also have sent a copy of the ITI form to ACAS (see page 134).

Conciliation
A conciliation officer from ACAS has a duty to try to bring about a peaceful settlement between the parties, which would avoid the need for the complaint to be heard by a tribunal. The conciliation officer will get in touch with both

sides promptly. The conciliation officer's job is to act as go-between if the parties indicate that they may be able to settle the matter: he is not there to advise either party on the merits or demerits of their cases. Things said to him are in the strictest confidence and will not be passed on to the other side without your permission. Likewise, nothing you have said can be used as evidence at a tribunal without permission. Remember that if you are prepared to enter into negotiations with the other side about a settlement, do so behind the shield of the phrase 'without prejudice' put at the top of any letter or declared before any discussions. This prevents the details and contents of any negotiations being mentioned at the hearing. Before accepting or refusing a settlement think the matter over very carefully. Ask yourself what you hope to gain from the hearing. Consider the respondent's case as well as your own. Many people get so single-minded about the strength of their own case that they forget that the other side may have strong arguments too.

If no settlement is reached, the case will be heard before an industrial tribunal on the date fixed unless you apply for a postponement. You are entitled to do this providing you have reasonable grounds such as other important commitments or one of your witnesses' inability to attend on that day.

If you do want to postpone the hearing write to the tribunal explaining your reasons and asking for a new date to be set. This is the type of letter you might write:

Dear Sir/Madam,   [Date]

Re. Wright v. Jacksons Ltd. – To be heard on [date]

I am writing to ask formally for a postponement of this case as [give reasons, for example: my main witness Mr Head is going to be abroad on the date fixed].
I would be most grateful if you would therefore postpone the case until after [date] when Mr Head will have returned.
I have informed the Respondents in writing that I have asked for a postponement.

Yours sincerely, Basil Wright

You must of course write a similar letter to the respondent.

Preparing your case for the tribunal
Draft a summary of your case. This is for your benefit and will be a constant source of reference during the hearing itself. It should include:

- **Details about your employment** When you started, your duties, qualifications, experience, your wages (take a pay packet/payslip for reference), details of overtime, the organisation of the firm etc. This will all be of great

159

importance to the tribunal as it will provide a background against which to examine the main body of your complaint

- **What went wrong** In this section make notes on all of the matters directly related to your complaint, details of any important interviews, who was there, what was said, the date etc
- **The law** Make a note of the law on which you are basing your claim (the legal advice you should have taken and the leaflets you have read will help you)
- **What you want** If you are claiming compensation, make a list of everything you are claiming for. Note too that you can claim compensation for abstract things such as general upset because of the whole business. If you are claiming compensation for expenses incurred in looking for another job, you are entitled to do so, but be careful to keep track of how much you spend on doing this as well as details of all the jobs. The tribunal will want to make sure that you have made a genuine attempt to get other work
- **Witnesses** Make a list of the witnesses you want to call to support your case. If they are unwilling to do so apply to the tribunal for a 'witness order' – this is an order compelling a particular person to attend as a witness – but bear in mind that a reluctant witness might turn out to be a bad witness. Once you have finalised your list of witnesses, note down the questions you intend to ask each one. Don't assume that you will think of the right questions on the day. Preparation is often the deciding factor between success and failure
- **Documents** You may believe that certain documents in the possession of someone else, for example an employer, are important to your case. Obviously you will want to see them in time to study them before the hearing. Make a list and write to the person holding them to release them. If you do not receive them you can ask the tribunal to make an order for **discovery and inspection** – in other words order the party specified to make available certain documents for your inspection

No amount of written guidance on the procedure at an industrial tribunal and the way in which to present your case can be a substitute for going to one and watching the proceedings. If you expect to see wigs, gowns, judges and juries, you are in for a disappointment. The industrial tribunal is not a Court – everything is far more informal. Three people hear the cases, one being the Chairman in charge of the whole proceedings.

The hearing

On the day of the hearing, you will be nervous, but if you have thought the matter through time and time again, and have made and taken notes, you can at least take comfort in the fact that you are thoroughly prepared.

The case will begin with you, the applicant, outlining your case and calling your witnesses, who will then be cross- and re-examined. Your employers, the respondent, will then present their case following the same principles. Finally you will both be given the opportunity to sum up, with you having the final say.

The decision
In many cases the tribunal's decision is announced by the Chairman there and then, along with the reasons for the decision, but sometimes you may have to wait for the decision in writing.

If you win the tribunal has the power to award a number of remedies.

- It can make an order declaring what the legal rights and wrongs are.
- It can recommend what steps are to be taken to put matters to rights, for example to give an unfairly dismissed employee his job back.
- It can award compensation – a monetary award often based on a rather complicated formula which takes into account the person's age, current earnings and length of service. The amount that can be paid varies according to the type of case.

If you are dissatisfied with the tribunal's decision
Both the applicant and the respondent have the right to appeal against the decision of the industrial tribunal, but only on a point of law, not on a matter of fact. The appeal must be made in writing to the Employment Appeal Tribunal within 42 days of the issue of the written summary of the tribunal's decision. If you are considering an appeal take advice before doing so, but don't hesitate once you have made up your mind.

Another way of showing your dissatisfaction with the tribunal's decision is to ask for a 'review'. This means that the tribunal will look closely at its own decision with a view to amending it. A review will only take place in certain limited circumstances, for example where proper notice of the tribunal hearing was not sent to one of the parties, where new evidence has come to light, or where there has been some error on the part of the tribunal staff. If you believe that there are grounds for a review to take place, you can either apply to the tribunal immediately after the decision has been given, or you have fourteen days after the date on which the tribunal's decision is sent to you to make a written request. Both the Department of Employment and ACAS publish helpful leaflets on the mechanics of the industrial tribunal.

Notes: Scotland and Northern Ireland

1 **Scotland**: claims of up to £1,000 are dealt with in the Sheriff Court under the Summary Cause Procedure; this may be used in claims for repossession of an article in connection with defective goods, and also the tenancy of a house.

A form of summons and a service document can be obtained from the Sheriff Clerk's office in person or by post. A leaflet is issued by the Scottish Information

Office on behalf of the Scottish Courts Administration to help you. Copies can be obtained from the Sheriff Clerks' Office or from your local Citizens Advice Bureau. The staff at the Sheriff Clerk's Office will explain the procedure to you, but for advice about your particular case you should go to the Citizens Advice Bureau or to a solicitor. You may be represented in Court by a non-lawyer if you wish, subject to the Court's approval. You should ask for this when your case first comes to Court.

Under Summary Cause, the expenses of the person who wins usually have to be met by the loser. Legal aid is available. If you conduct your case in person, and are successful, you should be able to recover reasonable outlays, including travel and loss of earnings for yourself and any witnesses.

Northern Ireland: Arbitration is also available for small claims in the County Court in Northern Ireland but the maximum amount is £300. The plaint fees are £4 for claims up to £75 and £10 for claims up to £300.

The booklet *Small Claims – The New Procedure in Northern Ireland* is available from the Citizens Advice Bureau.

2 The responsible government Department in Northern Ireland is the Department of Economic Development for Northern Ireland. The Labour Relations Agency (see page 134) will help you fill in the various forms if you decide to take your case to an industrial tribunal at the Central Office of the Industrial Tribunals.

3 In Scotland the Legal Advice Scheme is also known as the Pink Form Scheme.

Where to get help

Although this is primarily intended as a self-help book, in that it attempts to make you aware of how you can handle personal complaints and disputes yourself without the need for professional or expert advice, it is not meant as a substitute for such guidance. There may be cases calling for expert advice and positive assistance, and the best way of helping yourself is to seek such professional expertise. However at the end of the section there are some ideas for helping yourself.

THE LEGAL PROFESSION

The professional services of a lawyer can be expensive but so can the services of any professional or highly skilled person. However unlike the latter the services of a solicitor or barrister can often be obtained completely free or at a reduced rate through the Legal Aid and Advice Schemes, both available for civil cases only. They are publicly funded schemes to help the less well off pay for any legal expenses. The scheme is administered by the Law Society.[1]

Legal Advice (Green[1] Form Scheme)

If you need the assistance of a solicitor over a non-court case, for example to obtain general advice on some legal point, or to get him to write letters on your behalf to someone you are in dispute with, the Legal Advice (Green Form) Scheme is the one you need to know about. At its simplest it is a means-tested scheme whereby if you come within certain narrow financial limits you can get general advice from a solicitor, or get him to do certain work on your behalf, up to the value of £40, or £75 in undefended divorce cases. If it is necessary for a solicitor to do more work for you, the scheme can be extended, maybe even to provide another £40 or £75 worth of work. Note that if Court action becomes necessary the Legal Advice Scheme will not cover this and Legal Aid should be applied for.

How to apply and qualify for Legal Advice under the Green Form Scheme

In most cases you will not have to do anything as the solicitor will complete the 'green form' based on the information you give him. He will then tell you how much you have to pay (if anything). Not all solicitors take on work under the scheme so make sure about the one you are seeing, if you think you might qualify for help. Solicitors who operate the scheme usually have this sgn in their window:

Whether or not you can get help under the Green Form Scheme is totally dependent on a calculation which takes into account your **disposable income** and **disposable capital**. At its simplest, disposable income is what is left from a person's earnings (husband's and wife's are taken together) after certain deductions have been made to allow for tax, national insurance payments, mortgage or rent payments, and also after an allowance for any children has been made. If your disposable income is above a specified sum a week, you cannot get any help under the Green[1] Form Scheme, but if it falls below the figure you are entitled to help unless your disposable capital is above a certain limit. This is what is left after the total value of your assets has been added together, and the value of your house, furniture and the tools of your trade has been deducted. Depending on these calculations you may either get free legal advice, or merely have to make an appropriate contribution.

The solicitor himself can work out your entitlement under the scheme, as can the Citizens Advice Bureau or your Law Centre who can also provide you with a free leaflet on the scheme giving you the up-to-date figures and amounts involved.

Legal Aid

This scheme is for people involved in a Court case who feel that their own financial resources are inadequate when it comes to paying for legal fees. The Legal Aid Scheme begins where the Legal Advice Scheme ends: Court work cannot be handled by a lawyer under the Legal Advice Scheme. Whether or not you qualify for Legal Aid depends on two factors:

- **a means test** to determine whether you fall within certain financial limits
- **your case** – this must be looked at very carefully to determine whether or not it warrants public funds being spent on it

Give credit where credit is due and say thank you.

The means test

The means test for the Legal Aid Scheme is based on a similar formula to the one for the Legal Advice Scheme in that it takes into account disposable income and capital, but the figures which form the various financial limits are different. A free leaflet setting out the figures is available from the Citizens Advice Bureau. Your entitlement will be established and the means test conducted by the Supplementary Benefits Commission.

Your case

It has to be established that your case is one that merits public money being spent on it. It would be unjustifiable to spend taxpayers' money on a case of no public interest, or one that was doomed to failure before it even got to Court. A committee of the local Law Society will look at your case and if they think that you have a reasonable chance of success, and that you may actually gain something from the action, they will grant Legal Aid. If you are refused Legal Aid, you have the right to appeal to a special appeals committee of the Law Society.

The relevant application forms can be obtained from the Citizens Advice Bureau or from your solicitor. Both will be willing to advise you how to complete the forms in the most advantageous way – don't forget that your solicitor may do this under the Legal Advice Scheme.

This section has set out brief details of the Legal Aid and Advice Schemes only as far as civil cases are concerned. Legal Aid is available in some criminal cases too but is administered by the Court hearing the case and not the Law Society.

The fixed fee interview

This is a different scheme altogether from the Legal Aid and Advice Schemes: a solicitor will give the client a half-hour interview for the flat fee of £5. The purpose of this, as far as the client is concerned, is that in the half-hour he may get some idea of whether or not the case is worth pursuing. He will also be able to form an impression of the solicitor if they haven't met before. As far as the solicitor is concerned, it amounts almost to an introductory offer through which he hopes to get the client's business, and he can of course establish in the time whether the client has a case. The only drawbacks to the scheme are that it may take much longer than half an hour to assess the case, and that not all solicitors operate this scheme (although a very large proportion of them do). A word of caution before producing your fiver at the end of a half-hour interview: make sure that the solicitor knows the basis on which you are seeing him before you start, otherwise you may end up by finding that you are charged at the normal rate. A list of solicitors operating this scheme can be obtained from the Citizens Advice Bureau.

Choosing a solicitor

A particular solicitor may have done work for you or someone in your family before, maybe even years ago, so you regard him as your family solicitor. However, if you haven't already got a solicitor, there are a number of ways of finding one:

Recommendations Solicitors are prohibited from advertising so word-of-mouth recommendations are often their bread and butter. Ask your family, friends, colleagues.

The Legal Aid List is a list of all the solicitors who do work on the Legal Aid and Advice Schemes – your local library and the Citizens Advice Bureau keep a list. Apart from giving the name of the firm, it mentions briefly the kind of work each undertakes – many solicitors specialise in certain areas of the law and you may well want someone who is a particular specialist.

The Yellow Pages list solicitors but you will have to ring individually to find out the sort of work they specialise in.

WHERE ELSE TO GET HELP

Apart from the legal profession there are other bodies and organisations you can often turn to for help. Some of them offer their services free of charge.

Citizens Advice Bureau

This organisation can give advice on most legal issues arising on a daily basis – consumer law, employment law, family law, social benefit law and so on. There is no charge for advice and usually no appointment is necessary. All you do is go to the CAB office and make your enquiry. There are nearly 900 offices around the country, with at least one in every town or city. Their main function is to give general advice and assistance although occasionally they may actively take up a case on your behalf. If they feel they can't help they will always suggest where you can turn to. In many branches local solicitors give free legal advice once a week.

Trading Standards Departments

These are run by local authorities and provide free general advice on consumer law. They will occasionally actively take up a consumer's case. In some counties or regions the service goes by the name of Consumer Advice Centre or Consumer Protection Department but these are merely alternative titles for the Trading Standards Department.[2]

Law Centres

These places exist only in some parts of the country. They are generally free although some clients may be asked for a contribution. They often tend to deal with the problems affecting the needy, and their offices tend to be situated in less well-off areas. You should be able to find out about them from your local library or Citizens Advice Bureau.

Legal Advice Centres

Such places are similar in organisation to law centres but they will only give advice and will not usually undertake Court work.

Consumers' Association (Which? Personal Service)

Consumers' Association runs a personal service which gives legal advice and help on consumer matters. For an annual subscription, subscribers can submit their problems to a team of lawyers who will help and advise them until the case is resolved.

Prevention is better than cure so always think twice before buying goods and services and from whom you buy them.

HOW TO HELP YOURSELF

Demonstrations
It is perfectly legal to organise and to hold a demonstration. However before dashing out into the streets with banners you should note that in order for the demonstration to stay legal it must be peaceful and must not be held in a prohibited place. Ask the police's advice before holding a demonstration or large public meeting.

Petitions
If you believe that a large number of people share your sense of grievance about a particular issue a petition is possibly the best way to show that feeling. If nothing else several hundred or thousand voices making the same complaint may convince the body you are petitioning that the issue is worth more serious consideration. A petition does not need to be in formal language but usually starts with the phrase 'We the undersigned' with a very brief statement outlining the complaint. People should then be asked to sign their name, address, and their occupation.

Publicity
All too often individuals and organisations are more concerned about their public image than with anything else. With this in mind make sure you notify the local or even national press about your demonstration or petition. A letter to the News Editor will usually do the trick. Many local newspapers, radio stations and television programmes run phone-ins and feature items dealing exclusively with people who have problems in getting their complaint dealt with sympathetically.

Company annual general meetings
If you are a member or shareholder of a company you have the right to attend the annual general meeting. This provides you with an excellent opportunity to air your views if you have a complaint about the company or the way it is being run.

COMPLAINING TO THE EUROPEAN COURT OF HUMAN RIGHTS

If you feel that you are being deprived of your basic human rights and freedom and have unsuccessfully exhausted all possible legal remedies to obtain them or prevent them from being violated further, you still have one ace card – complain to the European Commission on Human Rights.

In November 1950 a number of European Ministers met in Rome and signed the European Convention on Human Rights. This amounts to a contract under which each of the states involved takes on certain obligations and duties involving recognition that individuals have certain basic rights. There are provisions that allow a national of one of the contractual states who feels his rights have been violated to commence proceedings using the specially set-up machinery in order to obtain some redress.

Rights protected by the Convention

- the right to life
- the right to liberty and security of person
- the right to fair administration of justice
- respect for private and family life, home and correspondence
- freedom of thought, conscience and religion
- freedom of expression and opinion
- freedom of peaceful assembly and association, including the right to join a trade union
- the right to marry and found a family
- the right to peaceful enjoyment of possessions
- certain rights to education
- liberty of movement and freedom to choose where to live
- the right to leave a country including one's own

Acts prohibited under the Convention

- torture and inhuman or degrading treatment and punishment
- slavery, servitude and forced labour
- retroactive criminal laws
- discrimination in the enjoyment of rights and freedoms guaranteed by the Convention
- expulsion by a state of its own nationals or denial of their entry
- the collective expulsion of aliens

If you feel that you have been deprived of any of your basic rights and freedoms you are entitled to go to the European Commission on Human Rights.

How to complain

- Check first that you have exhausted all effective and available legal remedies. The Commission will not take on your complaint unless you can satisfy them on this point.
- Write to the European Commission in Strasbourg for an application form on which to set out your complaint.

Alternatively you can simply submit your application without the appropriate form as long as you include:

- your name, age, address and occupation
- the name, address and occupation of anyone representing you
- the name of the state against which your complaint is brought
- the object of the application and if possible provisions of the Convention alleged to have been violated
- a statement of the facts and why you claim there has been a violation
- any relevant documents, in particular copies of any judgements or decisions given in your case by the state's Courts or administrative authorities

Your application must be made within six months of a final decision by the Courts or authorities which have heard your case.

What happens to your complaint?

The Commission decides first whether or not your complaint is admissible. They will check that you have exhausted all other remedies locally and have submitted a proper application within the specified six months. Of the three to four hundred applications made each year, about 90 per cent are inadmissible for various reasons. In order for the Commission to make a decision about a complaint's admissibility it may need further details and information from all parties concerned. If the application is regarded as inadmissible, that is the end of the matter: there is no appeal. If the application proves acceptable, the Commission will try to bring about a friendly settlement between the parties, based on a mutual respect for the objectives of the Convention.

If no settlement is reached, a full and detailed report is drawn up by the Commission, stating its opinions on whether or not there has been a breach of the Convention. This report goes both to the Committee of Ministers and to the State complained against. If the matter is still not settled, it is likely that the case will be referred to the European Court of Human Rights.

The seven judges there will examine all the documents and other evidence and may question the parties involved. After the hearing the judges will decide according to the majority view whether or not there has been any breach of the Convention.

The Court can order compensation as well as any costs to be paid to the injured party. In addition, it can recommend that the offending state take steps to see that a similar violation of the Convention does not occur again. There is no right of appeal.

How much does it all cost?

Basically nothing. There is no fee for making a complaint; your expenses will be met if you are called as a witness, and the Commission is in a position to provide free legal aid in certain circumstances.

Some examples of cases

The following are examples of issues raised in some forty cases that have come before the Court:

- restrictions on prisoners' rights of correspondence and rights of access to the Court
- use of the birch as judicial corporal punishment
- detention of vagrants without the opportunity for them to challenge their detention before a Court
- delays in bringing those on remand to trial
- delays in judicial and administrative proceedings
- requiring defendants in criminal cases to pay the cost of interpreters' fees
- denial of access to a Court where Legal Aid is available
- the legality of a trade union 'closed shop'
- corporal punishment in schools
- trade union freedoms to bargain collectively
- seizure and forfeiture of an obscene book
- compulsory sex education in schools
- controls of telephone tapping
- rights of transsexuals to change their status
- punishments for breaches of military discipline
- rights of mentally abnormal offenders to have their detention reviewed
- disciplinary proceedings against doctors

Notes: Scotland and Northern Ireland

1 In Scotland the services of an advocate can often be obtained free through the Legal Aid and Advice Schemes. The Legal Advice scheme is also known as the Pink Form Scheme, and is administered by the Law Society of Scotland.

   In Northern Ireland you can get 'Green Form' advice and assistance to the value of £40 (more in special circumstances if authority has been received from the Legal Aid department). Legal Aid is available for most divorce cases.

2 The Trading Standards Department is known in Northern Ireland as the Trading Standards Branch of the Department of Economic Development for Northern Ireland.

Addresses

Action for Victims of Medical Accidents
135 Stockwell Road,
London SW9 9TN
(01) 737 2434

Advertising Standards Authority
Brook House, 2–16 Torrington Place,
London WC1E 7HN (01) 580 5555

Advisory Centre for Education (ACE)
18 Victoria Park Square, London
E2 9PB
(01) 980 4596

Advisory, Conciliation and Arbitration Service (ACAS)
HEAD OFFICE
11–12 St James's Square, London
SW1Y 4LA
(01) 214 6000
NORTHERN
Westgate House, Westgate Road,
Newcastle upon Tyne NE1 1TJ
(0632) 612191
YORKSHIRE AND HUMBERSIDE
Commerce House, St Albans Place,
Leeds LS2 8HH
(0532) 431371
SOUTH EAST AND LONDON
Clifton House, 83–117 Euston Road,
London NW1 2RB
(01) 388 5100
SOUTH WEST
16 Park Place, Clifton, Bristol BS8 1JP
(0272) 211 921
MERSEYSIDE
Cressington House, 249 St Mary's
Road, Garston, Liverpool L19 0NF
(051) 427 8881

MIDLANDS
Alpha Tower, Suffolk Street,
Queensway, Birmingham B1 1TZ
(021) 643 9911
MIDLANDS
66–72 Hounsgate, Nottingham
NG1 6BA
(0602) 415450
NORTH WEST
Boulton House, 17–21 Chorlton
Street, Manchester M1 3HY
(061) 228 3222
SCOTLAND
Franborough House, 123–157
Bothwell Street, Glasgow G2 7JR
(041) 204 2677
WALES
Phase One, Ty Glas Road, Llanishen,
Cardiff CF4 5PH
(0222) 762636

Age Concern
ENGLAND
Bernard Sunley House, 60 Pitcairn
Road, Mitcham, Surrey CR4 3LL
(01) 640 5431

Air Transport Users' Committee
129 Kingsway, London WC2B 6NN
(01) 242 3882

Approved Coal Merchants Scheme
2 Turnpin Lane, Greenwich, London
SE10 9JA
(01) 853 0787
NORTH EASTERN
c/o National Coal Board, Consort
House, Waterdale, Doncaster
DN1 3HR
(0302) 66611

NORTH WESTERN
c/o National Coal Board, Anderton
House, Newton Road, Lowton,
Warrington, Lancashire WA3 2AG
(0942) 672404 x 245

NORTHERN
c/o National Coal Board, Coal House,
Team Valley Trading Estate,
Gateshead, Tyne & Wear NE1 1 0JD
(0632) 878822 x 6462

SOUTH WALES
242 S The Exchange, Mount Stuart
Square, Cardiff CF1 6ED
(0222) 32159

LONDON AND SOUTH EASTERN
505 Northern Road, South Harrow,
Middlesex HA2 8JP
(01) 864 0535

EASTERN
The Building Centre, 15–16
Trumpington Street, Cambridge
CB2 1QD
(0223) 63058

SOUTHERN
28 Broad Street, Wokingham, Berks
RG11 1AB
(0734) 783930

SOUTH WESTERN
40 Tyndalls Park Road, Clifton,
Bristol BS8 1PL
(0272) 730648

MIDLANDS
Fuel House,
1 Vicarage Lane, Water Orton,
Birmingham B46 1RY
(021) 748 1049

NORTH MIDLANDS
16 Pelham Road, Sherwood Rise,
Nottingham NG5 1AY
(0602) 621520

SCOTLAND
9 Atholl Place, Edinburgh EH3 8HP
(031) 229 4836

**Architects' Registration Council of
the United Kingdom (ARCUK)**
73 Hallam Street, London W1N 6EE
(01) 580 5861

Associated Scottish Life Offices
23 St Andrews Square, Edinburgh
EH2 1AQ
(031) 556 7171

**Association of British Travel Agents
(ABTA)**
55–57 Newman Street, London
W1P 4AH
(01) 637 2444

Association of Certified Accountants
29 Lincoln's Inn Fields, London
WC2A 3EE
(01) 242 6855

**Association of Manufacturers of
Domestic Electrical Appliances
(AMDEA)**
593 Hitchin Road, Stopsley, Luton
LU2 7UN
(0582) 412444

Association of Optical Practitioners
233–234 Blackfriars Road, London
SE1 8NW
(01) 261 9661

Banking Information Service
10 Lombard Street,
London EC3V 9AR
(01) 626 8486

Bar Council, The
11 South Square, Grays Inn, London
WC1R 5EL
(01) 242 0082

Barclays Bank PLC
Head Office, 54 Lombard Street,
London EC3P 3AH
(01) 636 1567

Belfast Education and Library Board
40 Academy Street, Belfast BT1 2MQ
(0232) 229211

British Broadcasting Corporation
Broadcasting House, Portland Place,
London W1A 4WW
(01) 580 4468

**British College of Ophthalmic
Opticians**
10 Knaresborough Place, London
SW5 0TG
(01) 373 7765

British Decorators' Association
45 Sheen Lane, London SW14 8AB
(01) 876 4415
British Gas Corporation
National Westminster House,
326 High Holborn, WC17 3DP
(01) 242 0789
British Insurance Association
Aldermary House, 10–15 Queen
Street, London EC4N 1TU
(01) 248 4477
**British Insurance Brokers'
Association (BIBA)**
Fountain House, 130 Fenchurch
Street, London EC3M 5DJ
(01) 623 9043
British Rail Regional Offices
EASTERN
The Railway Station, York YO1 1HP
(0904) 53022
LONDON/MIDLAND
Euston House, Eversholt Street,
London NW1 1BG
(01) 387 9400
SCOTTISH
Buchanan House, 58 Port Dundas
Road, Glasgow G4 0HG
(041) 332 9811
SOUTHERN
Waterloo Station, London SE1 8SE
(01) 928 5151
WESTERN
Paddington Station, London
W2 1HA
(01) 723 7000
British Railways Board
Melbury House, Melbury Terrace,
London NW1 6JU
(01) 262 3232
British Telecom
2–12 Gresham Street, London
EC2 7AG
(01) 432 1234
British Telecom
Churchill House, 20 Victoria Square,
Belfast BT1 4QA
(0232) 242424

**Broadcasting Complaints
Commission, The**
20 Albert Embankment, London
SE1 7TL
(01) 211 8465
Building Societies Association, The
34 Park Street, London W1Y 3PF
(01) 629 7233
Central Office of Industrial Tribunals
93 Ebury Bridge Road, London
SW1 8RE
(01) 730 9161
Central Office of Industrial Tribunals
2nd Floor, Bedford House, 16/22
Bedford Street, Belfast BT2 7NR
(0232) 227666
Central Office of Information
Hercules Road, London SE1 7DU
(01) 928 2345
Central Services Agency (N.I.)
25 Adelaide Street, Belfast BT2 8FH
(0232) 224431
**Central Transport Consultative
Committee for Great Britain**
3–4 Great Marlborough Street,
London W1V 2EA
(01) 439 6901
Chartered Institute of Arbitrators
75 Cannon Street, London
EC4N 5BH
(01) 236 8761
**Chartered Institute of Public Finance
and Accountancy**
1 Buckingham Place, London
SW1E 6HS
(01) 828 7661
Child Poverty Action Group
1 Macklin Street, Drury Lane,
London WC2B 5NH
(01) 242 9149
Children's Legal Centre, The
20 Compton Terrace, London
NW1 2UN
(01) 359 9392
Citibus Ltd
Milewater Road, Belfast BT3 9BG
(0232) 745201

Citizens Advice Bureaux, National Association of,
110 Drury Lane, London WC2B 5SW
(01) 836 9231

Coal Advisory Service (N.I.)
87 Eglantine Avenue, Belfast BT9 6EW
(0232) 681331

Commission for Racial Equality, The
Elliot House,
10–12 Allington Street,
London SW1E 5EH
(01) 828 7022
BIRMINGHAM
Stanier House,
10 Holliday Street, Birmingham B1 1TQ
(021) 632 4544
LEEDS
133 The Headrow, Leeds LS1 5QX
(0532) 434413
LEICESTER
Haymarket House,
Fourth Floor,
Haymarket Shopping Centre,
Leicester LE1 3YG
(0533) 57852
MANCHESTER
Maybrook House, Fifth Floor, 40
Blackfriars Street, Manchester M3 2EG
(061) 831 7782

Commissioner for Administration
Office of the Northern Ireland
Parliament, 33 Wellington Place,
Belfast BT1 6HN
(0232) 233821

Commissioner for Complaints (N.I.)
Progressive House, 33 Wellington
Place, Belfast BT1 6HN
(0232) 233821

Commissioners for Local Administration (Local Government Ombudsmen)
GREATER LONDON, SOUTH EAST,
SOUTH WEST, WEST MIDLANDS, EAST
ANGLIA
21 Queen Anne's Gate, London
SW1H 9BU
01 222 5622

NORTH AND EAST MIDLANDS
29 Castlegate, York YO1 1RN
(0904) 30151
SCOTLAND
5 Shandwick Place, Edinburgh
EH2 4RG
(031) 229 4472
WALES
Derwen House, Court Road,
Bridgend, Mid-Glamorgan
CF31 1BN
(0656) 61325

Companies Registration Office
Companies House, 55–71 City Road,
London EC1Y 1BB
(01) 253 9393
(personal callers only; no correspondence)
Companies House, Crown Way,
Maindy, Cardiff CF4 3UZ
(0222) 388588
(correspondence only; no personal callers)

Companies Registration Office (N.I.)
43/47 Chichester St, Belfast BT1 4RJ
(0232) 234121

Confederation for the Registration of Gas Installers (CORGI)
St Martins House, 140 Tottenham
Court Road, London W1P 9LN
(01) 387 9185

Consumers' Association
14 Buckingham Street, London
WC2N 6DS
(01) 839 1222

Customs and Excise Department
Kings Beam House, 39–41 Mark
Lane, London EC3R 7HE
(01) 283 8911

Department of Economic Development for Northern Ireland
Netherleigh, Massey Avenue, Belfast
BT4 2JP
(0232) 63244

Department of Education and Science
Elizabeth House, 39 York Road,
London SE1 7PH
(01) 928 9222

Department of Employment
Caxton House, Tothill Street, London
SWIH 9NS
(01) 213 3000

Department of Energy
Thames House South, Millbank,
London SWIP 4QJ
(01) 211 3000

Department of the Environment
2 Marsham Street, London SWIP 3EB
(01) 212 3434

**Department of the Environment for
Northern Ireland**
Parliament Building, Stormont, Belfast
BT4 3SY
(0232) 63210

**Department of the Environment for
Northern Ireland** (*Planning Division*)
Commonwealth House, 35 Castle
Street, Belfast BTI 1GH
(0232) 221212

**Department of the Environment for
Northern Ireland** (*Rating Division*)
Oxford House, 49 Chichester Street,
Belfast BTI 4JD
(0232) 235211

**Department of Health and Social
Security**
Alexander Fleming House, Elephant
and Castle, London SEI 6BY
(01) 407 5522

Department of Trade
1 Victoria Street, London SWIH 0ET
(01) 215 7877
(Civil Aviation Policy Division)
(01) 215 3856

Domestic Coal Consumers' Council
2 Bunhill Row, London ECIY 8LL
(01) 638 8914

**Electrical Contractors' Association,
The (ECA)**
ESCA House, 32–34 Palace Court,
London W2 4HY
(01) 229 1266

**Electrical Contractors' Association of
Scotland, The**
23 Heriot Row, Edinburgh EH3 6EW
(031) 225 7221

Electricity Consultative Councils
EASTERN
8 Arcade Street, Ipswich IPI 1EJ
(0473) 58355

EAST MIDLANDS
Caythorpe Road, Lowdham,
Nottingham NGI4 7EA
(0602) 3208

LONDON
Room 159, 4 Broad Street Place,
Blomfield Street, London
EC2M 7HE
(01) 638 4803

MERSEYSIDE AND NORTH WALES
3rd Floor, Martins Bank Buildings,
Exchange Street West, Water Street,
Liverpool L2 3SA
(051) 236 8681

MIDLANDS
Shawton House, 794 Hagley Road
West, Oldbury, Warley, West
Midlands B68 0PJ
(021) 422 8087

NORTH EASTERN
Room 103, Centro House, Cloth
Market, Newcastle upon Tyne
NEI 1UA
(0632) 322780

NORTH WEST
Longridge House, Corporation Street,
Manchester M4 3AJ
(061) 834 4362

SOUTHERN
8a St Mary's Butts, Reading, Berkshire
RGI 2LN
(0734) 599657

SOUTH EASTERN
1 Boyne Park, Tunbridge Wells, Kent
TN4 3EL
(0892) 20947

SOUTH WALES
Caerwys House, 36 Windsor Place,
Cardiff CFI 5UF
(0222) 26093

SOUTH WESTERN
Northernhay House, Northernhay
Place, Exeter, Devon EX4 3RL
(0392) 58968

177

YORKSHIRE
The Woodlands, Wetherby Road,
Scarcroft, Leeds LS14 3HR
(0532) 892038

Electricity Consumers' Council, The
Brook House, 2–16 Torrington Place,
London WC1E 7LL
(01) 636 5703

Electricity Council, The
30 Millbank, London SW1T 4RD
(01) 834 2333

Employment Appeal Tribunal
4 St James's Square, London
SW1Y 4JU
(01) 214 3367

Equal Opportunities Commission
Overseas House, Quay Street,
Manchester M3 3HN
(061) 833 9244
Caerwys House, Windsor Place,
Cardiff CF1 1LB
(0222) 43552
249 West George Street, Glasgow
G2 4QE
(041) 226 4591

**European Commission on
Human Rights**
Council of Europe, Avenue de
l'Europe, 67006 Strasbourg Cedex,
France
(010 33) 88 614 961

Footwear Distributors' Federation
Commonwealth House, 1–19 New
Oxford Street, London WC1 1PA
(01) 404 0955

Gas Consumers' Council
SCOTTISH
86 St George Street, Edinburgh
EH2 3BU
(031) 226 6523
NORTHERN
18 Fawcett Street, Sunderland,
Tyne and Wear SR1 1RH
(0783) 74272/41007
NORTH WESTERN
Boulton House, Chorlton Street,
Manchester M1 3HY
(061) 236 1926

NORTH EASTERN
3rd Floor, National Deposit House,
1 Eastgate, Leeds LS2 7RL
(0532) 39961
EAST MIDLANDS
2 Salisbury Road, Leicester LE1 7QR
(0533) 551560
WEST MIDLANDS
Broadway House, 60 Calthorpe Road,
Five Ways, Edgbaston, Birmingham
B15 1TH
(021) 454 5510
WALES
St David's House, Wood Street,
Cardiff CF1 1ES
(0222) 26547
EASTERN
51 Station Road, Letchworth, Herts
SG6 3BQ
(046 26) 5399
NORTH THAMES
8 Bulstrode Street, London W1M 5FT
(01) 487 2666
SOUTH EASTERN
Helena House, 348 High Street,
Sutton, Surrey SM1 1QA
(01) 642 1127
SOUTHERN
2a Holdenhurst Road,
Bournemouth, Dorset BH8 8AJ
(0202) 26654
SOUTH WESTERN
Royal Building, St Andrew's Cross,
Plymouth, Devon PL1 2DS
(0752) 667707

General Dental Council
37 Wimpole Street, London W1M 8DQ
(01) 486 2171

General Medical Council
44 Hallam Street, London W1N 6AE
(01) 580 7642

General Optical Council
41 Harley Street, London W1N 2DJ
(01) 580 3898

**Gingerbread Association for One
Parent Families**
35 Wellington Street, London WC2E 7BN
(01) 240 0953

Guild of Dispensing Opticians
22 Nottingham Place, London
WIM 4AT
(01) 935 7411

Health Service Commissioner (Ombudsman) for England and Northern Ireland
The Office of the Parliamentary Commissioner and Health Service Commissioner,
Church House, Great Smith Street, London SWIP 3BW
(01) 212 7676

Health Service Commissioner (Ombudsman) for Scotland
2nd Floor, 11 Melville Crescent, Edinburgh EH3 7LU
(031) 225 7465

Health Service Commissioner (Ombudsman) for Wales
4th Floor, Pearl Assurance House, Greyfriars Road, Cardiff CF1 3AG
(0222) 394621

Independent Broadcasting Authority
70 Brompton Road, London SW3 1EY
(01) 584 7011

Industrial Life Offices Association
Aldermary House, 10–15 Queen Street, London EC4N 1TL
(01) 248 4477

Inland Revenue
Somerset House, Strand, London WC2R 1LB
(01) 438 6622

Institute of Chartered Accountants in England and Wales
Chartered Accountants Hall, Moorgate Place, London EC2P 2BJ
(01) 628 7060

Institute of Chartered Accountants of Ireland (ULSTER BRANCH)
11 Donegal Square South, Belfast BT1 5JE
(0232) 221600

Institute of Chartered Accountants of Scotland
27 Queen Street, Edinburgh EH2 1LA
(031) 225 5673

Institute of Chartered Secretaries and Administrators
16 Park Crescent, London W1N 4AH
(01) 580 4741

Institute of Cost and Management Accountants
63 Portland Place, London W1N 4AB
(01) 580 6542

Institute of Plumbing
Scottish Mutual House, North Street, Hornchurch, Essex RM11 1RU
(040 24) 45199

Insurance Brokers' Registration Council
15 St Helens Place, London EC3A 6DS
(01) 588 4387

Insurance Ombudsman Bureau
31 Southampton Row, London WC1B 5HJ
(01) 242 8613

Labour Relations Agency
(NORTHERN IRELAND)
Windsor House, 9/15 Bedford Street, Belfast BT2 7NU
(0232) 221442

Lands Tribunal
(FOR NORTHERN IRELAND)
Royal Courts of Justice (Ulster), Chichester Street, Belfast BT1 3JJ
(0232) 235111

Law Centre, The
(FOR NORTHERN IRELAND)
62 Bedford Street, Belfast BT2 7FH

Law Society, The
(FOR ENGLAND AND WALES)
113 Chancery Lane, London WC2A 1PL
(01) 242 1222
(FOR SCOTLAND)
26–27 Drumsheugh Gardens, Edinburgh EH3 7YR
(031) 226 7411
(FOR NORTHERN IRELAND)
Royal Courts of Justice, Chichester Street, Belfast BT1 3JZ
(0232) 231614

Law Society, The
(FOR NORTHERN IRELAND) Law
Society House, 90–106 Victoria
Street, Belfast BT1 3JZ
(0232) 231614

Lay Observer, The
Room 265, Royal Courts of Justice,
Strand, London WC2A 2LL
(01) 405 7641

Lay Observer for Northern Ireland
IDB House, 64 Chichester Street,
Belfast BT1 4LE
(0232) 233233

Lay Observer for Scotland, The
22 Melville Street, Edinburgh EH3 7NS
(031) 225 3236

Life Offices Association
Aldermary House, 10–15 Queen
Street, London EC4R 1AD
(01) 248 4477

Linked Life Assurance Group
12–16 Watling Street, London
EC4M 9BB
(01) 236 0861

Lloyds Advisory Department
Lloyds New Building, 51 Lime Street,
London EC2M 7HJ
(01) 623 7100

Lloyds Bank PLC
71 Lombard Street, London EC3P 3BS
(01) 626 1500

Local Government Ombudsmen
– see Commissioners for Local
Administration

**London Transport Passengers'
Committee**
1 King Street, London WC2E 8HN
(01) 240 3701

**Mail Order Traders' Association of
Great Britain**
360–366 Oxford Street, London
W1N 0BT
(01) 493 9748

The Master (Taxing)
(Enforcement of Judgement Office)
7th Floor, Bedford House, Bedford
Street, Belfast BT2 7FD
Belfast (0232) 245081

Midland Bank PLC
Poultry, London EC2P 2BX
(01) 606 9911

**MIND (National Association for
Mental Health)**
22 Harley Street, London W1N 2ED
(01) 637 0741

Motor Agents' Association Ltd, The
201 Great Portland Street, London
W1N 6AB
(01) 580 9211

**National Association for Mental
Health (MIND)**
22 Harley Street, London W1N 2ED
(01) 637 0741

National Association of Estate Agents
Arbon House, 21 Jury Street, Warwick
CV34 4EH
(0926) 496800

**National Association of Retail
Furnishers**
17/21 George Street, Croydon, Surrey
CR9 1TQ
(01) 680 8444

National Bus Company
172 Buckingham Palace Road,
London SW1W 9TN
(01) 730 3453

National Express
Digbeth Coach Station, High Street,
Digbeth, Birmingham B5 6DQ
(021) 622 4373

**National Federation of Building
Trades Employers**
82 New Cavendish Street, London
W1N 8AD
(01) 580 5588

National Gas Consumers' Council
5th Floor, Estate House, 130 Jermyn
Street, London SW1Y 4UJ
(01) 930 7431

National Holidays
Mill Street East, Dewsbury, West
Yorkshire WF12 9AG
(0924) 451041

National House Building Council
58 Portland Place, London W1N 4BU
(01) 637 1248

National Inspection Council for Electrical Installation Contractors
237 Kennington Lane, London
SE11 5QJ
(01) 582 7746

National Planning Aid Unit
c/o Town and County Planning Association, 17 Carlton House Terrace, London SW1Y 5AS
(01) 930 8903

National Tenants' Organisation
c/o David Archer, 7 Galba Court, Augustus Close, Brentford, Middx
(01) 568 5415

National Westminster Bank PLC
Head Office, 41 Lothbury, London
EC2P 2BP
(01) 606 6060

Newspaper Publishers' Association Ltd
6 Bouverie Street, London EC4Y 8OY
(01) 583 8132

Newspaper Society, The
Whitefriar House, 6 Carmelite Street, London EC4Y OBL
(01) 583 3311

Northern Ireland Consumers' Council
176 Newtonbreda Road, Newtonbreda, Belfast BT8 4QS
(0232) 647151

Northern Ireland Electricity Consumers' Council
Stranmillis Embankment, Belfast
BT9 5FN
(0232) 661825

Northern Ireland Electricity Service
120 Malone Road, Belfast BT9 5HT
(0232) 661100

Northern Ireland Housing Executive
2 Adelaide Street, Belfast BT2 8BA
(0232) 240588

Northern Ireland Post Office Users' Council
3rd Floor, Chamber of Commerce House, 22 Great Victoria Street, Belfast BT2 7PU
(0232) 244113

Northern Ireland Railways
Central Station, East Bridge Street, Belfast BT1 3PD
(0232) 230310

Northern Ireland Schools Examination Council
42 Beechill Road, Belfast
BT8 4QN
(0232) 704666

Northern Ireland Transport Users' Committee
Hampden House, 55 Royal Avenue, Belfast BT1 1TX
(0232) 244174

Office of Fair Trading
Field House, 15–25 Bream's Buildings, London EC4A 1PR
(01) 242 2858

One Parent Families, National Council for
255 Kentish Town Road, London
NW5 2LX
(01) 267 1361

Parliamentary Commissioner and Health Service Commissioner (Ombudsman)
Church House, Great Smith Street, London SW1P 3BW
(01) 212 7676

Patients Association, The
Room 33, 18 Charing Cross Road, London WC2H OHR
(01) 240 0671

Periodical Publishers' Association Ltd
Imperial House, 15–19 Kingsway, London WC2B 6UN
(01) 836 9204

Pharmaceutical Society of Great Britain
1 Lambeth High Street, London
SE1 7JN
(01) 735 9141

Pharmaceutical Society of Northern Ireland
73 University Street, Belfast
BT7 1HL
(0232) 226927

Police Authority for Northern Ireland, The
River House, 48 High Street, Belfast
BT1 2BE
(0232) 230111

Police Complaints Board
Waterloo Bridge House, Waterloo
Road, London SE1 8UT
(01) 275 3236

Post Office
(Headquarters), 2 St Martins le
Grand, London EC1A 1PG
(01) 432 1234

Post Office Users' National Council
(POUNC)
Waterloo Bridge House, Waterloo
Road, London SE1 8UA
(01) 928 9458

Press Council, The
1 Salisbury Square, London EC4Y 8AE
(01) 353 1248

Radio, Electrical and Television Retailers' Association (RETRA)
RETRA House, 57–61 Newington
Causeway, London SE1 6BE
(01) 403 1463

Royal Association for Disability and Rehabilitation (RADAR)
25 Mortimer Street, London W1N 8AB
(01) 637 5400

Royal Courts of Justice (NORTHERN IRELAND)
Chichester Street, Belfast BT1 3JJ
(0232) 235111

Royal Institute of British Architects (RIBA)
66 Portland Place, London W1N 4AD
(01) 580 5533

Royal Institution of Chartered Surveyors
12 Great George Street, Parliament
Square, London SW1P 3AD
(01) 222 7000

Royal Ulster Constabulary
Brooklyn, Knock Road, Belfast
BT5 6LD
(0232) 650222

Scottish Bus Group
Carron House, 114–116 George
Street, Edinburgh, EH2 4LX
(031) 226 7491

Scottish Daily Newspapers' Society
50 George Square, Glasgow G2 1RR
(041) 552 4994

Scottish Development Department
New St Andrews House, St James
Centre, Edinburgh EH1 3SZ
(031) 556 8400

Scottish Examination Board
Ironmills Road, Dalkeith, Mid Lothian
EH22 1LE
(031) 663 6601

Scottish House Furnishers' Association
203 Pitt Street, Glasgow G2 4DB
(041) 332 6381

Scottish Motor Trade Association Ltd
3 Palmerston Place, Edinburgh
EH12 5AQ
(031) 225 3643

Scottish Newspapers' Proprietors Association
Edinburgh House, 3–11 North St
Andrew's Street, Edinburgh
EH2 1JU
(031) 557 3600

Secretary of State for England,
Department of Education and Science
Elizabeth House, York Road, London
SE1 7PH
(01) 928 9222
SCOTLAND
Department of Education, New St
Andrew's House, St James' Centre,
Edinburgh EH1 3SY
(031) 556 8400
WALES
Crown Buildings, Cathays Park,
Cardiff CF1 3NQ
(0222) 82511

Secretary of State for Wales
Welsh Office, Gwydyr House,
Whitehall, London SW1A 2ER
(01) 233 3000

Shelter, National Campaign for the Homeless
157 Waterloo Road, London SE1 8UU
(01) 633 9377
Society of Motor Manufacturers and Traders Ltd, The
Forbes House, Halkin Street, London SW1X 7DS
(01) 235 7000
Society of Opticians
63 Great Cumberland Place, Bryanston Square, London W1H 7LJ
(01) 723 9556
Solid Fuel Advisory Service
Hobart House, Grosvenor Place, London SW1X 7AE
(01) 235 2020
Stock Exchange, The
Old Broad Street, London EC2
(01) 588 2355
Stock Exchange, The
(NORTHERN IRELAND)
Northern Bank House, 10 High Street, Belfast BT1 2BP
(0232) 221094

Ulsterbus Ltd
Milewater Road, Belfast BT3 9BG
(0232) 745201
Ulster Furniture Federation
2 Greenwood Avenue, Belfast BT4 3JL
(0232) 656275
Vehicle Builders' and Repairers' Association
Belmont House, 102 Finkle Lane, Gildersome, Leeds LS27 7TW
(0532) 538 333
Welsh Office
Crown Buildings, Cathays Park, Cardiff CF1 3NQ
(0222) 825111
Welsh Office Planning Division
Crown Buildings, Cathays Park, Cardiff CF1 3NQ
(0222) 82511

Index

INDEX

A Handbook of Consumer Law

This is a layman's guide to the subject compiled by the National Federation of Consumer Groups. The book uses specific examples to illustrate the principles of consumer law and the way in which they are likely to be interpreted in the courts. Areas covered include: advice on buying, defective goods and services, unsolicited goods, consumer credit, consumer safety, trade descriptions and labelling, contracts and liabilities.

Raising the Money to Buy Your Home

Whether you are a first-time buyer or wanting to take out another mortgage for the new home you are buying, this book takes you through the choices that face you and explains the differences between interest rates, mortgage terms and limits on loans offered by different lenders. There are tables and calculations to help you work out how much you are actually paying and the cost of repayment mortgages. Applying for a loan is described, as is how to get a top-up loan and what to do about paying off a mortgage.

The Legal Side of Buying a House

A house is probably the most expensive item that anyone is likely to buy in their life. To save some of the cost – solicitors' fees – this handbook explains the legal processes of buying an owner-occupied house with a registered title in England or Wales (not Scotland). It takes you step by step through a typical house purchase, and also deals with the legal side of selling a house.

The Which? Book of Saving and Investing

This detailed guide gives advice on using saving and investment opportunities to achieve specific ends, perhaps an early retirement or a child's education. It explains, amongst other matters, what to do with a legacy, how to save the money to buy a home in the most efficient way, how to reduce your tax bill on spare-time earnings, how to choose a building society and in general how to manage your money in the most profitable way.

Starting Your Own Business

Whether you want to put a lifetime's training and experience to work for you or hope to turn a spare-time interest into a profitable business, or just want to be independent, this book shows you how to set about it. It covers choosing the kind of business to set up; psychological and practical preparation; raising capital; starting a company; finding premises; advertising and marketing; insurance; staff; accounts and taxes; the legal aspect of retailing and being an employer; planning ahead and expansion. The book also lists governmental and other agencies which offer help to the aspiring businessman.

Earning Money at Home

This is for anyone who has to stay at home and would like to make some money at the same time. The book explains what this entails in the way of organising domestic life, family and children, keeping accounts, taking out insurance, coping with tax, costing, dealing with customers, getting supplies. It suggests many activities that could be undertaken, with or without previous experience.

What to Do When Someone Dies

This is a sympathetic and practical handbook which provides explanations of doctor's certificates, deaths reported to the coroner and what this entails, registering a death and getting the various certificates that may be needed afterwards. Differences between burial and cremation procedures are discussed, and the arrangements that have to be made, mainly through the undertaker, for the funeral. The book details the various national insurance benefits that may be claimed.

Wills and Probate

In this companion *What to Do When Someone Dies*, information and guidance are given about the administration of an estate by executors, without the help of a solicitor. It explains clearly about filling in the necessary forms, the valuation of the estate, what is involved in obtaining probate, payment of fees and CTT, and the distribution of the estate. It also shows, with examples, how to prepare a will so as to take advantage of any CTT exemptions. The final section deals with intestacy.

All these publications are available from Consumers' Association, Castlemead, Gascoyne Way, Hertford SG14 1LH.